Section Six — The Exam

D0493727

Section Seven — Creative Writing

Section Eight — The Controlled Assessment — English Language

Section Nine — The Controlled Assessment — English

Published by CGP

Editors:
Claire Boulter
Polly Cotterill
Katherine Craig
Edmund Robinson
Edward Robinson
Caley Simpson
Jennifer Underwood
Sarah Williams

Contributors:
Caroline Bagshaw
Fiona Ingram
Peter Inson
Ian Miles
Wendy Novak
Elisabeth Sanderson
Nicola Woodfin

With thanks to Carl Dowling, Rachael Powers and Emma Willshaw for the proofreading.

ISBN: 978 1 84146 929 4

Groovy website: www.cgpbooks.co.uk

Jolly bits of clipart from CorelDRAW®
Printed by Elanders Ltd, Newcastle upon Tyne.

Based on the classic CGP style created by Richard Parsons.

How to Use this Book

This book will help you with the writing questions of your GCSE English/English Language exam. The writing questions are in section B of the Unit 1 exam. There's one question on 'informative or descriptive writing', and one question where you write to 'argue and persuade'. The last few sections will help you with the Unit 3 controlled assessment, where you have to do some creative writing.

The Assessment Objectives tell you what Skills you need

The assessment objectives are the things that AQA say you need to be able to do to get good marks for these bits of the GCSE. Don't worry — there aren't very many of them. Put simply, you have to:

1) Write clearly and imaginatively, using the appropriate language and form for your audience.

2) Organise your ideas into sentences, paragraphs and whole pieces of text, using a range of writing techniques and structures. This will make sure your ideas are well linked and easy to understand.

3) Use a variety of sentence structures, and use good punctuation and spelling.

Each Section of the book deals with a Different Skill

SECTION 1 is about the purpose (why you're writing), the audience (who you're writing for) and the form (whether you're writing a letter, article or advert etc).

SECTION 2 is about how to write to inform and explain.

SECTION 3 is about writing to describe.

Sections 1-7 are for both the English and English Language GCSEs.

SECTION 4 tells you how to write to argue and persuade.

SECTION 5 tells you how to write to advise.

SECTION 6 contains some example "producing non-fiction texts" questions for the writing part of the Unit 1 exam. It also shows you the mark scheme for the exam, and some sample answers, working from a C grade up to an A*.

SECTION 7 is about creative writing.

SECTION 8 tells you about the Controlled Assessment you have to do if you're doing GCSE English Language, and gives you some sample answers (from a C grade up to an A*).

SECTION 9 tells you about the Controlled Assessment you have to do if you're doing GCSE English, and gives you some sample answers (from a C grade up to an A*).

At the end of the book there's a handy glossary that gives you definitions of loads of important words and terms that you might need.

The book also doubles up as a rather fetching hat...

This book is full of straightforward ways of getting extra marks. Read through the explanations and examples and practise all the tips individually. Then try to include as many as you can in your work.

The Purpose of the Text

The writing exam questions will always tell you the <u>purpose</u> of the text you have to write — in other words, <u>why</u> the text is being written. The purpose gives you clues about what <u>style</u> to use.

The Purpose is given in the Question

1) The question will tell you the reason you're writing the text. For example:

> Choose a time when you have been very angry and explain why you felt that way.

Here's the purpose.

2) The purpose tells you how your writing should <u>affect</u> your reader. Choose your <u>details</u> and <u>language</u> to create the right effect.

3) Think about the <u>purpose</u> of your writing when you start <u>planning</u> your answer — and make sure your finished piece matches your purpose <u>all</u> the way through.

Each Exam Question focuses on different writing Purposes

You have to answer <u>two</u> different questions in your exam.

1) The first writing task involves <u>informative</u> or <u>descriptive</u> writing, e.g.

> Write a letter to a friend explaining why you want to get a pet.

This question is fairly <u>short</u>, and will probably include <u>details</u> of <u>your own experiences</u>.

2) The second writing question wants you to <u>take a particular viewpoint</u>, e.g.

> Some people think that teenagers should be taught to look after their finances at school. Write an article arguing for or against this idea.

This question is a bit <u>longer</u> — you need to keep up your <u>argument</u> all the way through.

Sometimes a question has More than one Purpose

There could be a question in the exam with <u>more than one</u> purpose, e.g.

> Write a letter to a local business arguing that schools need more support and persuading them to help.

Make sure you cover <u>both</u> purposes in your answer.

Every question has at least one porpoise.

My life has no purpose — and nor does my essay...

The techniques you use to write for each purpose often overlap. Have a look at the next few sections in this book for help with matching your writing style to the purpose in the question.

The Purpose of the Text

Your writing must <u>suit its purpose</u> all the way through to get the <u>high grades</u>. It might seem like a lot of effort, but <u>it's really worth it</u>. Here are some important areas to work on.

Structure your writing to suit the Purpose

Work out the best <u>structure</u> for your answer. It depends on what you want your writing to <u>achieve</u>. Writing to <u>persuade</u> the council should be structured differently from writing to <u>advertise</u> spot cream.

Here's an example of an exam question. And here's one way the answer to this particular question could be <u>structured</u>:

> Write an article for your school paper in which you argue that teenagers are given a bad press.

1) Start by stating the problem.
2) Then give some examples of unfair reports and attitudes.
3) Go on to say why they're wrong.
4) Give some positive examples.
5) Finish with what you want to happen now.

Teenagers are often given a bad dress.

Choose your language Carefully

The language you use has to suit your <u>purpose</u>. For example, your letter to the council should be <u>formal</u> and <u>serious</u>, but your advert for spot cream can be <u>chatty</u> and <u>fun</u>. No matter what you're writing though, your <u>vocabulary</u> needs to be '<u>sophisticated</u>' to get the top grades. Make sure you're using language that'll get you plenty of marks:

This shows the audience is other teenagers.

Like me, you must be weary of the incessant criticism. We're intelligent and aware young citizens with a mature understanding of the issues threatening our planet. Why are we ignored?

Words like this show off your vocabulary.

Use a rhetorical question (see p32) to get your audience involved.

Adapt techniques for Different Purposes

1) Good writing techniques work really well for all sorts of <u>purposes</u> — you just need to <u>adapt</u> them. E.g. you can use <u>questions</u> in loads of ways:

> PERSUADE A HEAD TEACHER — "What would you say to a 100% success rate for your students?"

> INTRODUCE AN EXPLANATION — "How does the money help?"

> ADVISE TEENAGERS — "So what's the big deal about road safety?"

> DESCRIBE A FEAR — "What is it that grips my heart in an icy clutch?"

2) Use a range of details to suit your purpose. E.g. if you're writing to <u>persuade</u>, include some <u>emotive examples</u> and <u>shocking statistics</u>. If you're writing to <u>describe</u> put in details from <u>all five senses</u>.

Choose your language — but it's gotta be English...

Structure structure structure. I simply can't say it enough. (Well, maybe 3 times is enough for one page, but you get my drift...). MAKE SURE YOU STRUCTURE YOUR ANSWER PROPERLY. End.

The Audience

Sometimes the questions will tell you <u>who</u> you're writing for (the <u>audience</u>). Writing for teenagers is different from writing for your ancient and cantankerous head teacher. Oh yes.

Vary your writing Style to match your Audience

Work out who your <u>audience</u> is <u>before</u> you start writing, and think about what <u>style</u> you need to use:

> Write a report for your school governors which persuades them to allow changes to your school uniform.

Keep the tone of your writing <u>formal</u>. School governors would expect a <u>professional</u> approach.

If you're writing for a <u>teenage</u> audience, you can probably be more <u>informal</u>.

> Adults often criticise the way teenagers dress. Advise teenagers on how to respond to this criticism.

Sometimes a question has <u>more</u> than one audience for you to deal with:

> Write a letter to a magazine called 'Adventure Holidays' arguing for or against adventure holidays for children.

Your letter will be addressed to the <u>editor</u> of this magazine, but you're <u>also</u> writing for the <u>readers</u>, who may have mixed opinions.

Questions Don't always tell you Who the audience is

1) The <u>first</u> writing question (inform or describe) <u>might not</u> say who the writing is for. If that happens, just assume you're writing for the <u>examiner</u>.

2) The <u>second</u> writing question (argue or persuade) nearly always <u>tells</u> you <u>who</u> the audience is.

> If you could choose, where in the world would you like to live? Explain the reasons for your choice.

There's no obvious <u>audience</u>, so write your answer to the <u>examiner</u> here.

Impress your audience — boast about your new bike...

You might think a speech for your school assembly would be informal as you're addressing fellow students, but think about it more carefully... If it's about a serious subject, then you might be better off making your speech more formal. There's more about all this on the next few pages.

The Audience

Matching your <u>writing style</u> to your <u>audience</u> is very important. Here are a few points to remember.

Don't make your Writing too Simple

1) If the question asks you to write to a <u>friend</u>, don't write too casually and <u>never</u> use <u>text talk</u>.
2) You can sound <u>chatty</u> but make sure you still include a <u>range</u> of sentences and vocabulary.
3) Being <u>sarcastic</u> or <u>humorous</u> can help you write 'to a friend' without writing too simply.
4) Remember, you have to <u>show off</u> your writing skills — keep it chatty, but don't get <u>carried away</u>.

This is the sort of thing you <u>should</u> be writing:

> *Of course I'm grateful that they allow me to slave tirelessly into the early hours of the morning.*

Here are some examples of <u>what not to do</u>:

> *His fiery, pungent, yet fragrant, aromatic odour reverberated resonantly in my vibrating nostrils.*

This is a bit over the top and ridiculous.

> *Mate, here's some goss 4 ya. That guy from skool u like stank like 2 much BO 2day.*

No no no no. Absolutely not. Don't do this.

You may have to Write in Character

Sometimes you have to pretend to be an <u>expert</u> at something. Try to get in <u>character</u> a bit, but don't worry — you won't need lots of <u>specialist knowledge</u>.

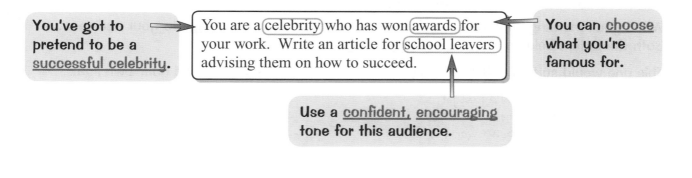

You've got to pretend to be a <u>successful celebrity</u>.

You are a (celebrity) who has won (awards) for your work. Write an article for (school leavers) advising them on how to succeed.

You can <u>choose</u> what you're famous for.

Use a <u>confident</u>, <u>encouraging</u> tone for this audience.

You're a brain surgeon — write an instruction manual...

The reason people sometimes come unstuck in English exams is because they weren't prepared. The earlier you learn all this stuff the easier you'll find it in the exam. You'll have time to get in plenty of practice in advance so it shouldn't be too scary when you're faced with the real thing.

Form — Letters

There are lots of different <u>forms</u> you could be asked to write in... You might be asked to write a leaflet, a magazine article, a speech etc. This page is about writing a <u>letter</u>.

Some Letters need to be Formal

1) If the question asks you to write a <u>letter</u>, look at the <u>audience</u> to see if it needs to be formal. If it's to people you don't know well, or to people in positions of <u>authority</u>, keep it <u>formal</u>, e.g.

> Write a letter to the head of a national charity, explaining how your school wants to help fundraise.

2) Start with a formal <u>greeting</u>, e.g. 'Dear Sir/Madam' or 'Dear Mrs Jones'. <u>Sign off</u> formally too — '<u>Yours sincerely</u>' if you've used their <u>name</u>, '<u>Yours faithfully</u>' if you <u>haven't</u>.

3) Use <u>standard</u> English and <u>formal</u> vocabulary — don't get too chatty:

So cheers, mate, thanks a lot for all your help. It's been a laugh eh?

> Don't use language like this in a formal letter — it's just too casual.

> This is much better — lots of impressive formal language.

In conclusion, Prime Minister, I would like to assure you that we are most grateful for your support in our campaign. The project has been a challenging yet rewarding one.

> Sentences like this create an impersonal tone, which sounds more professional.

Informal Letters are more Relaxed

A letter to a <u>friend</u> or <u>relative</u>, or someone your own age should have a more <u>informal</u> tone.

1) Start with your reader's <u>name</u>. Sign off with 'best wishes' or 'see you soon'.

2) You can <u>assume</u> the reader already knows certain things about you:

> I'm sure you'll remember how I feel about spiders. Well this was ten times worse.

Don't overdo it though — stick to the <u>main point</u> of the letter.

3) When you're writing informally, you've still got to match your <u>language</u> to your audience. Both the letters below are giving <u>informal advice</u>.

This one would suit an <u>elderly relative</u>:

> Anyway, I thought I'd just jot down a few tips to help you cope with the journey. Don't worry — I'm sure it'll be fine!

This one is for a <u>friend</u> your own age:

> Here it is then: my handy guide to spending eight hours on a plane and still looking gorgeous at the other end.

Dear Mum, I've forgotten how to do exams...

What you say and how you say it is more important than getting the layout right. You don't need to worry about putting addresses on your letter or anything. Just concentrate on using the right tone to suit your audience — and that goes for other forms of writing like articles and leaflets too.

Form — Adverts, Leaflets and Articles

Adverts, leaflets and articles are forms which come up quite often in exam questions. Here are some of the basic rules about writing them. They don't let you draw things or colour in — the meanies.

Organise your text

When you're writing an advert, leaflet or article, you can use headings, subheadings (see p17) and bullet points to make your writing more effective. Make sure your paragraphs are well developed though — don't split your writing into too many short sections.

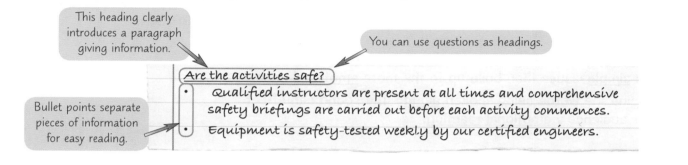

This heading clearly introduces a paragraph giving information.

You can use questions as headings.

Are the activities safe?
- Qualified instructors are present at all times and comprehensive safety briefings are carried out before each activity commences.
- Equipment is safety-tested weekly by our certified engineers.

Bullet points separate pieces of information for easy reading.

Adverts have got to be Persuasive

1) An advert could be advertising many different things, e.g. a product, a charity or even a political party.

2) Whatever you have to advertise, you've got to be persuasive. So use plenty of persuasive techniques to convince the reader that you're right.

3) The style of your advert should be very different depending on your audience and what you're advertising.

> Write the text for a mobile phone advertisement which aims to persuade young men to buy the phone.

Leaflets are often Informative

1) If you have to write a leaflet, you can write in paragraphs, but you can also include subheadings and bullet points.

2) You could be asked to write an informative leaflet, or one to explain or to advise.

3) Write in a style to suit your audience, but don't let it get too simple just because it's a leaflet.

> Write the text of a leaflet which informs tourists of what your area has to offer them.

Articles can have Different Purposes

1) An article can be for a magazine or a newspaper. The type of publication will give you important clues about what kind of audience you're writing for.

2) If you're asked to write an article, look carefully at the purpose. If the purpose is to inform, focus on who, what, when and where. If the purpose is to argue, focus on your point of view.

Be creative, darling...

Whatever kind of text you're writing, you only have to write the words for it — you won't get any extra marks for colouring in your heading or drawing a picture. This should be obvious from the question anyway — the questions always say "write the text for" rather than "make a leaflet".

Form — Other Types of Text

It's strange, but you might have to use the form of a <u>spoken text</u> for a writing question in the exam. You might be asked to write the text for a <u>speech</u> or a <u>radio broadcast</u>, or something like that.

You might have to write Speeches or Radio Scripts

1) <u>Speech</u> and <u>radio script</u> questions often ask you to <u>argue</u> or <u>persuade</u>.

> Write the text for a speech in which you persuade local shopkeepers to get more involved in recycling activities.

This means that you can use a whole range of <u>persuasive devices</u> (see pages 30-35).

2) <u>Structure</u> your writing to give it <u>dramatic impact</u>. E.g. start with <u>simple</u> issues then build up to the more <u>emotional</u> ones.

3) Imagine the words being spoken <u>aloud</u>. The sound can affect your audience's <u>emotional reaction</u>:

> These accusations are hateful, hurtful and humiliating.

Alliteration (see p17) and using a set of three adjectives make this statement sound strong and angry.

4) Use a range of <u>sentence structures</u> to make it sound like <u>spoken language</u>. Put in some <u>exclamations</u> and questions. Use <u>contractions</u> — 'we'll' and 'she's' instead of 'we will' and 'she is', to make the speech sound more <u>engaging</u> and <u>personal</u> to the audience. <u>Vary</u> the length of your sentences to show pauses and emphasis too.

Think about who your Audience is

1) If it's a speech, don't forget that you can talk <u>directly</u> to your audience. Use plenty of <u>personal pronouns</u> — 'I', 'you' and 'we'. Also refer to <u>why</u> everyone is there listening, e.g. "thanks for coming to show your support for this cause".

2) There are plenty of chances to <u>anticipate</u> your audience's responses. This always goes down well with the examiner because it shows you <u>understand</u> your audience's point of view.

> You are probably sitting there wondering what gives me the right to tell you how to run your businesses.

You're guessing what they're thinking so you can deal with their concerns.

Don't set out your writing like a Play Script

1) '<u>Write the text</u>' means don't worry about <u>fancy layout</u> — just write normally.

2) <u>Organise</u> your writing into clear, detailed <u>paragraphs</u>.

3) The examiner just wants to see if you can create the kind of writing that's <u>suitable</u> for this type of <u>audience</u> and <u>occasion</u>.

Darren could always anticipate his audience's response. If only it was less hurtful.

But I wanted to write a gritty crime drama...

...that'll be screened at 2am on BBC4, with a rugged, hard-nosed copper who never does things by the book forced to partner with an idealistic and naive young recruit. As the two track down a sadistic serial killer they slowly create a bond, and when the killer... whaddya mean, it's not original?

Exam Technique

You don't actually get marks for your plan, but if you spend a few minutes making one it'll help you write a <u>well-organised</u> and <u>thoughtful</u> answer. And that will get you <u>good marks</u>, of course.

Think about the Question...

<u>Underline</u> the key words in the question.

This is the <u>form</u> you're writing in.

Here's your <u>audience</u>. Be fairly <u>informal</u> but remember they may not have met you.

Write a <u>letter</u> to a <u>pen friend</u> in which you <u>explain</u> what your ambitions are for the future.

This is the <u>purpose</u> — you'll need to give plenty of details and <u>reasons</u>.

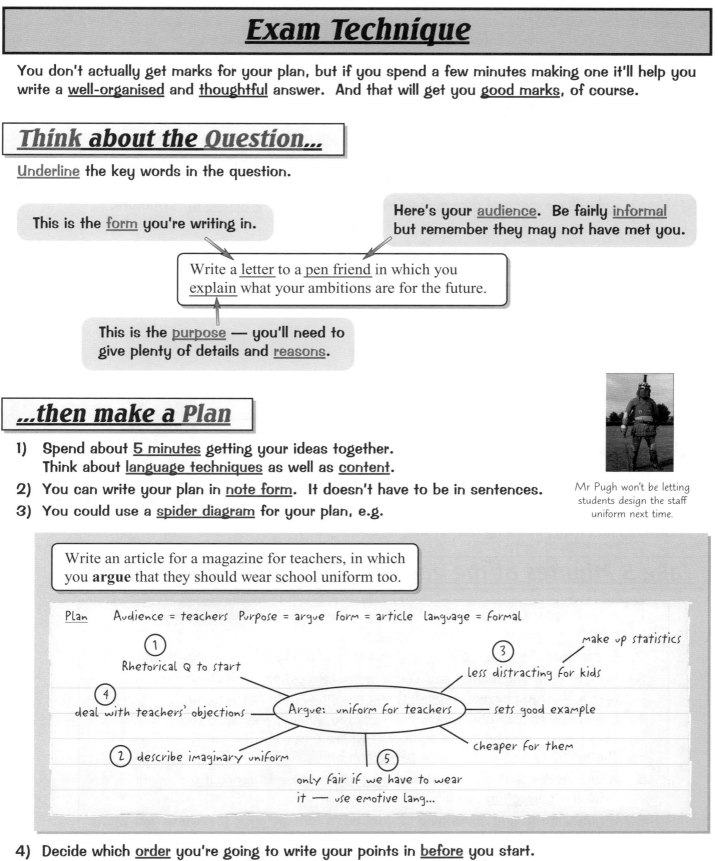

Mr Pugh won't be letting students design the staff uniform next time.

...then make a Plan

1) Spend about <u>5 minutes</u> getting your ideas together. Think about <u>language techniques</u> as well as <u>content</u>.

2) You can write your plan in <u>note form</u>. It doesn't have to be in sentences.

3) You could use a <u>spider diagram</u> for your plan, e.g.

Write an article for a magazine for teachers, in which you **argue** that they should wear school uniform too.

Plan   Audience = teachers   Purpose = argue   form = article   language = formal

① Rhetorical Q to start

③ less distracting for kids — make up statistics

④ deal with teachers' objections — Argue: uniform for teachers — sets good example

② describe imaginary uniform

cheaper for them

⑤ only fair if we have to wear it — use emotive lang...

4) Decide which <u>order</u> you're going to write your points in <u>before</u> you start. Don't forget — you'll need a strong <u>introduction</u> and <u>conclusion</u> too.

Plan an escape route from the exam hall...

Now it's time for some planning practice. Try writing plans for some of the example exam questions in Section Six. Try different types of plan, (invent your own method if you like) but don't spend more than 5 minutes on each one. There's much more about planning on the next page and p.12.

Exam Technique

There is no single right way to plan. So just choose the one that <u>suits you best</u>.

Choose your Structure

1) While you're making your <u>plan</u>, you should think about your writing's <u>structure</u>.

2) For example, you might want to mention some bits in more <u>detail</u> than others, or create a certain <u>effect</u> with your writing.

3) Here's a plan for a piece of <u>descriptive</u> writing which has a "<u>zooming in</u>" structure.

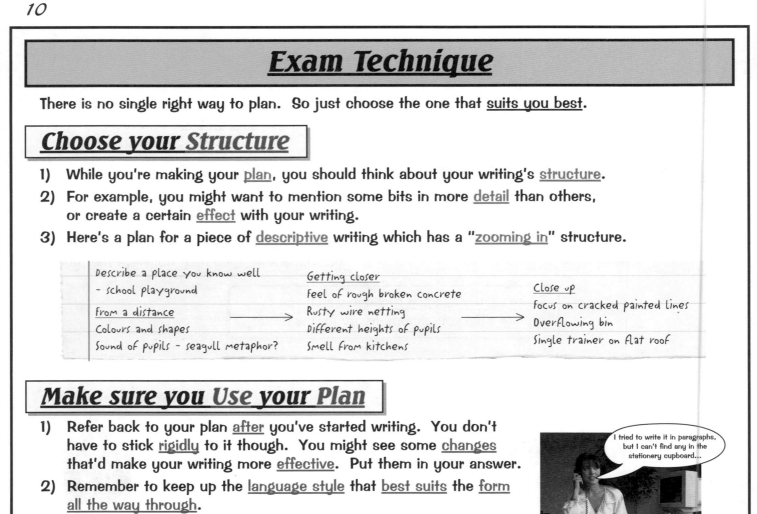

Describe a place you know well
– school playground

<u>From a distance</u>
Colours and shapes
Sound of pupils – seagull metaphor?

$\longrightarrow$

Getting closer
Feel of rough broken concrete
Rusty wire netting
Different heights of pupils
Smell from kitchens

$\longrightarrow$

<u>Close up</u>
Focus on cracked painted lines
Overflowing bin
Single trainer on flat roof

Make sure you Use your Plan

1) Refer back to your plan <u>after</u> you've started writing. You don't have to stick <u>rigidly</u> to it though. You might see some <u>changes</u> that'd make your writing more <u>effective</u>. Put them in your answer.

2) Remember to keep up the <u>language style</u> that <u>best suits</u> the <u>form all the way through</u>.

3) You must write in <u>paragraphs</u>. You also need to <u>link</u> them so that they all flow on from each other. Examiners call this '<u>coherent</u>' writing, and they're looking out for it.

I tried to write it in paragraphs, but I can't find any in the stationery cupboard...

Take 5 Minutes at the end to Check Your Work

1) Look at your <u>punctuation</u> and <u>spelling</u>. It's easy to make unnecessary mistakes when you're under <u>pressure</u>.

2) Check that the <u>opening</u> is <u>strong</u> and that you have a proper <u>conclusion</u>.

3) Look at your <u>vocabulary</u> and add in more <u>interesting</u> words if you can. Check that you haven't <u>repeated</u> any words without meaning to.

4) If you realise that you should have started a new paragraph, <u>show</u> the examiner by putting in the symbol // where you want the paragraph to end. The examiner will treat it as a <u>paragraph break</u>.

5) If you realise that you've made a <u>mistake</u>, it's fine to <u>cross it out</u> neatly and write the <u>correction</u> above.

6) If you want to <u>add</u> something in, just put a little <u>asterisk</u> (*) where you want to add something. Then put another asterisk in the margin and neatly write what you want to add.

Plans and structures — is this architecture or English?

Seriously though, don't panic when you see everyone else in the exam starting to write really fast straight away — they'll be writing rubbish. Take some time to read the questions carefully, pick the one you think you can answer best, then take 5 minutes to make a plan. It's the right way to do it.

Other Writing Tips

Here are some <u>more ideas</u> to help you prepare for the <u>writing questions</u>. I'm amazed at my own generosity in writing this page for you — no no, don't thank me — it's been a pleasure.

You Can Revise for English

Whatever people say, there <u>are</u> things you can do before the exam which will <u>improve</u> your writing paper marks — it's <u>not</u> all natural talent, y'know.

1) Learn a list of <u>connectives</u>. These are words that help you <u>start sentences</u> in <u>different</u> ways. They also help you <u>organise</u> your points clearly and make <u>links</u> between paragraphs more obvious.

> however   although   finally
> nevertheless   despite
> consequently   obviously

2) Memorise some <u>persuasive devices</u> (see pages 30-35) and <u>descriptive techniques</u> (pages 24-25). You can use them with a whole range of audiences and forms.

3) Practise writing <u>paragraphs</u> and <u>linking</u> them together. You could even write a one-sentence paragraph for real shock value. Only do it <u>once</u> in an essay though, or it'll lose its impact.

4) <u>Vary</u> your writing style. Use <u>short sentences</u> to add a sense of drama, then some nice long <u>flowing sentences</u> to change the <u>pace</u> of your writing.

Be Creative

1) Examiners want you to do <u>well</u>, and they're <u>looking out</u> for stuff to give you <u>marks</u> for. Have a go at things — don't be <u>shy</u> and think you'll look silly.

2) You get marks for your <u>language</u> and separate marks for <u>spelling</u> and <u>punctuation</u>. Try out interesting words, even if you're not completely confident using them.

No, not that sort of creativity... tsk.

3) What you write <u>doesn't</u> have to be <u>true</u>, even if the question says to write from personal experience. You can make things up or <u>exaggerate</u> and the examiner won't know or care, as long as you keep it realistic. They're only marking your <u>language skills</u>.

4) Use your <u>imagination</u> — don't just use really <u>obvious</u> words:

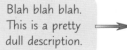
Blah blah blah. This is a pretty dull description.

> As I walked over the battlefield, I thought that I could still hear the cries of wounded men and smell the rotten flesh of the dead men. There were some apple trees and the field was very muddy.

> As my feet sank into the clay soil, it seemed to sigh with the last breaths of the fallen. The breeze brought the smell of the apple harvest from neighbouring orchards. The thick scent gave a hint of sweet corruption; the fetid ripeness of corpses, their bright uniforms blooming in the grass.

This is more interesting — comparing the corpses to rotting apples is much more inventive and paints a more vivid picture.

5) Feel free to invent <u>facts</u>, <u>statistics</u>, <u>examples</u> and <u>quotations</u> too. You'll get credit for using the <u>techniques</u>, even if the details aren't <u>true</u>.

Just make it up...

You need to control your writing, especially vocabulary and sentence structure. It's better to write two sides of carefully chosen words than to ramble on for pages. It's called 'conscious crafting'.

Planning Your Essay

You'll get marks for how well <u>structured</u> your answer is — so make sure you <u>plan</u> it first.

Plan your ideas using a Spider Diagram

When you're planning <u>what</u> you're going to write about, write down all your <u>ideas</u> so you don't forget any. Remember, you might find it helps to make a <u>spider diagram</u> like this one.

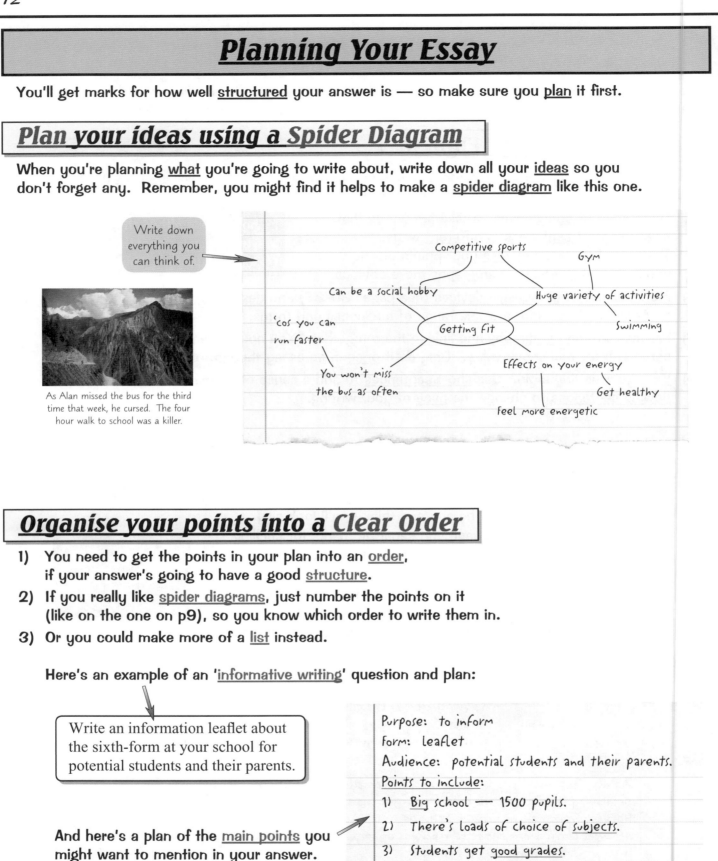

Write down everything you can think of.

As Alan missed the bus for the third time that week, he cursed. The four hour walk to school was a killer.

Competitive sports

Gym

Can be a social hobby

Huge variety of activities

'cos you can run faster

Getting Fit

Swimming

Effects on your energy

You won't miss the bus as often

Get healthy

feel more energetic

Organise your points into a Clear Order

1) You need to get the points in your plan into an <u>order</u>, if your answer's going to have a good <u>structure</u>.

2) If you really like <u>spider diagrams</u>, just number the points on it (like on the one on p9), so you know which order to write them in.

3) Or you could make more of a <u>list</u> instead.

Here's an example of an '<u>informative writing</u>' question and plan:

Write an information leaflet about the sixth-form at your school for potential students and their parents.

And here's a plan of the <u>main points</u> you might want to mention in your answer.

Purpose: to inform
Form: leaflet
Audience: potential students and their parents.
Points to include:
1) <u>Big</u> school — 1500 pupils.
2) There's loads of choice of <u>subjects</u>.
3) Students get <u>good grades</u>.
4) Great facilities e.g. 6th form <u>common room</u>.

Arachnophobes can do an octopus diagram instead...

Organising your ideas before you actually start writing your answer is a great idea. Having a good plan stops you waffling on about nothing when you could be writing a much better answer. It doesn't have to be really detailed — just outline the points you want your writing to include.

Spelling and Punctuation

You get <u>marks</u> for <u>spelling</u> and <u>punctuation</u> in the writing sections — so make your work as <u>accurate</u> as possible. Don't avoid hard words just because you might spell them wrong, though.

Punctuation affects Meaning and Style

1) You must use <u>commas</u> and <u>full stops</u> to make your writing clear.
    They're particularly important when you're writing <u>long sentences</u>:

> *Although it was raining, the pool, which reflected the moonlight at its edges, still preserved a glassy, unruffled surface, in which I could see the wavering shapes of the surrounding trees.*

2) <u>Apostrophes</u> can be tricky. Learn the <u>two main uses</u> and you'll be fine:

   - Put them where you've <u>missed out</u> letters: → *It's a shame we didn't realise she'd be there.*

   - Use them to show <u>possession</u>: → *The cat's fear increased as the children's footsteps got closer and the boys' shouts were heard.*

   If a possessive word is a <u>plural</u> and <u>already</u> ends in 's', just add an apostrophe <u>after</u> the 's'.

3) Use <u>semicolons</u> to create more <u>sophisticated</u> sentences (but don't use them in every sentence).
    They <u>separate</u> the ideas like a full stop does, but keep them in the <u>same sentence</u>:

> *It was freezing. Flakes of snow fell relentlessly from a blank, grey sky.*

Look how the semicolon makes a fancier sentence. →

> *It was freezing; flakes of snow fell relentlessly from a blank, grey sky.*

4) Check that you've put ! and ? where you need them,
    especially if you've written a <u>speech</u> or an <u>informal</u> piece.

Make your Spelling as Accurate as possible

1) You <u>don't</u> have to spell every single word right to get high marks — but you'll need to show you can get <u>some</u> of the more complicated ones right. Make your own <u>list</u> of words that you know you need to learn. Here are some tricky ones to get you started:

> argument conscience favourite immediately conscious necessarily
> occasional disappear embarrassed deceived unnatural

2) Learn the more common <u>homophones</u> (words that cause confusion because they <u>sound</u> the same):

THERE, THEIR and THEY'RE	<u>They're</u> going to have to take <u>their</u> coats off when they get <u>there</u>.
HERE and HEAR	I can't <u>hear</u> you from over <u>here</u>.
YOUR and YOU'RE	<u>You're</u> going to love <u>your</u> birthday present.
WE'RE, WHERE, WEAR and WERE	<u>We're</u> going to Malta, <u>where</u> we'll <u>wear</u> bikinis all day. We <u>were</u> going to go there last year, but we didn't.

A werewherewear wolf

The homophones sit next to the oboes...

I'd love to, but I haven't room here to tell you how to spell every word you might ever need.
Anyway, hopefully this page reminds you about the things you might need to learn before the exam.

SECTION ONE — PURPOSE, AUDIENCE AND FORM

Writing to Inform and Explain

When you write to <u>inform</u> you do what it says on the tin — you give people information. Similarly, writing to <u>explain</u> is giving people an explanation. It's not rocket science.

Writing to inform *Tells the reader Facts*

So what's this writing to inform business all about? Well...

1) Writing to inform means <u>telling</u> the reader something as <u>clearly</u> and <u>effectively</u> as possible.

2) You'll probably have to talk about <u>personal experiences</u>, e.g. a <u>significant incident</u> in your life. However, the emphasis will be on giving out clear <u>facts</u> rather than opinions and waffle.

There are <u>Loads</u> of different <u>Types</u> of <u>Writing to Inform</u>

Here are some <u>examples</u> of the sorts of thing you might have to write for an <u>inform</u> question:

1) A <u>magazine article</u> informing people about your <u>concerns for the planet</u>.
2) A <u>letter</u> to a <u>pen-friend</u> telling them about <u>where you live</u>.
3) A <u>personal account</u> of a <u>school or club event</u>.
4) A <u>leaflet</u> of <u>travel tips</u> for a journey across the Sahara, based on your own trip there.

Your style might be <u>formal</u> or <u>informal</u> — it depends on your <u>audience</u>.

Explanations *tell your audience Five Main Things*

The best way to "write to explain" is to tell your audience five <u>key points</u>:

| The WHAT... | ...the HOW... | ...the WHERE... | ...the WHEN... | ...and the WHY. |

In other words...

<u>What</u>'s going on, <u>how</u> it's happening, <u>where</u> and <u>when</u> it is, and <u>why</u> it's happening.

Explanations *can take many forms*

1) When you explain something, <u>break down the detail</u> of a topic to present it <u>clearly</u>. Just like revision, things are easier to understand when explained in smallish chunks.

2) Think carefully about <u>who</u> your writing is <u>aimed at</u> and <u>adapt</u> your writing style to this <u>audience</u>.

3) Here are a few <u>common types</u> of "writing to explain" question that you might get in your exam:

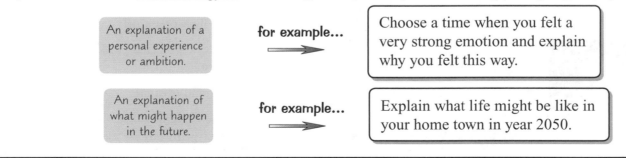

An explanation of a personal experience or ambition.

for example... → Choose a time when you felt a very strong emotion and explain why you felt this way.

An explanation of what might happen in the future.

for example... → Explain what life might be like in your home town in year 2050.

What? Why? How? Is this some sort of investigation...?

When you're writing to inform or explain, make a list of the main points of information you want to get across before you start. It'll make it a lot easier to structure your answer and make it interesting.

Audience and Form

So, you know a bit about <u>writing to inform</u> and <u>explain</u> now, and here's a page telling you some more. This is the second step on the ladder to becoming an evil genius and taking over the world. Maybe.

Think about your Audience...

1) Explaining a hobby to a friend is <u>very different</u> from explaining a business proposal to a company.
2) So you must remember to think about <u>who</u> you're writing for.
3) Then you can adapt what you're writing to make it <u>more relevant</u> and so <u>more interesting</u> to them.
4) Whoever you're writing for, you should still make sure your writing is <u>grammatically correct</u>.

...then Adapt your Content

Below are some questions and extracts of answers which are written using very <u>different styles</u>. Yep, you guessed it in one, the <u>style</u> used depends on the <u>audience</u>.

> Write a letter to your MP explaining what you know about people's opinions on crime in your area.

> As is clear from the statistics, the more people became aware of crime in their street, the more they became afraid. The most marked increase in fear was among the 65-75 age group.

← A formal and serious style.

> Write a letter to a friend explaining why you think that they would have enjoyed a holiday that you recently took.

> I've just arrived back from my break in Greece and I think you would have loved it. There was a good variety of watersports to try, and I know that would really suit you.

← An informal, chatty style.

Choose Language to fit your Audience and Form

Think about <u>who</u> you're writing for (the <u>audience</u>) and the <u>form</u> you're writing in (e.g. letter, article). Then <u>choose</u> your <u>language</u> to <u>fit</u> these, and get your <u>information</u> across.

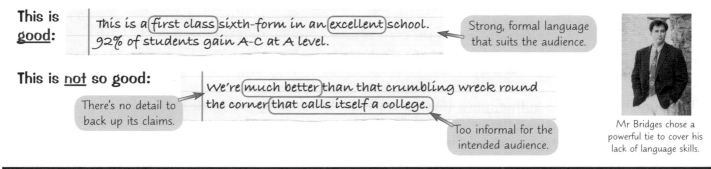

This is <u>good</u>:
> This is a first class sixth-form in an excellent school. 92% of students gain A-C at A level.

→ Strong, formal language that suits the audience.

This is <u>not</u> so good:
> We're much better than that crumbling wreck round the corner that calls itself a college.

There's no detail to back up its claims. →

Too informal for the intended audience.

Mr Bridges chose a powerful tie to cover his lack of language skills.

Well my audience is you — and I'm writing to explain...

...about making your writing suitable for your audience. If you're writing to someone important, don't use slang or silliness. However, if you're writing to a friend, you can be a bit more chatty.

Structure

Once you know <u>what</u> you want to say, you need to think about <u>how</u> to say it.

Start with an Introduction

When you're writing to inform or explain, whatever the topic, you should <u>begin</u> with a <u>paragraph</u> clearly setting out the <u>main points</u> you want to <u>get across</u> to your audience.

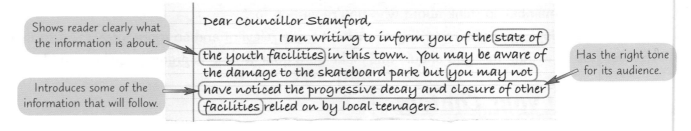

Shows reader clearly what the information is about.

Introduces some of the information that will follow.

Dear Councillor Stamford,
I am writing to inform you of the state of the youth facilities in this town. You may be aware of the damage to the skateboard park but you may not have noticed the progressive decay and closure of other facilities relied on by local teenagers.

Has the right tone for its audience.

Your writing needs to be Clearly Organised

Use <u>subheadings</u>, <u>lists</u>, <u>bullet points</u> and <u>paragraphs</u> to keep your writing <u>easy to follow</u>.

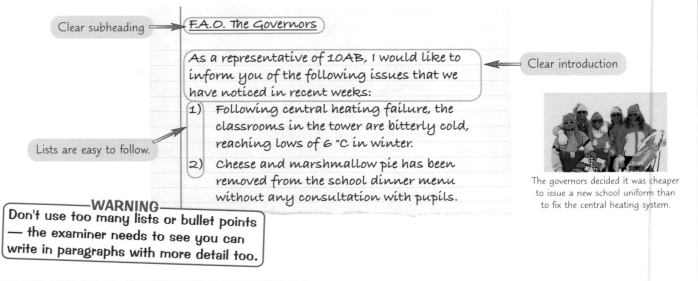

Clear subheading

F.A.O. The Governors

As a representative of 10AB, I would like to inform you of the following issues that we have noticed in recent weeks:

Clear introduction

1) Following central heating failure, the classrooms in the tower are bitterly cold, reaching lows of 6 °C in winter.

2) Cheese and marshmallow pie has been removed from the school dinner menu without any consultation with pupils.

Lists are easy to follow.

The governors decided it was cheaper to issue a new school uniform than to fix the central heating system.

—WARNING—
Don't use too many lists or bullet points — the examiner needs to see you can write in paragraphs with more detail too.

Build Up your explanation

A good explanation <u>builds up information</u> and <u>detail</u> so the reader can follow it easily.

A clear statement tells you what this paragraph will generally be about.

Most people don't drink enough water. Are you drinking enough? You need 6 to 8 glasses of water per day to clear the body of toxins and hydrate the cells. If you are dehydrated the cells become shrivelled and they do not function to their full capacity.

Here, some extra detail has been added.

There's even more detail here and 'if' has been used to talk about cause and effect.

This paragraph sounds <u>authoritative</u> (like an expert). You <u>believe</u> the facts in it because it sounds like the writer knows what they're talking about. This is the sort of thing you should be aiming for.

Key is organisation to writing good — well, sort of...

Your answers should be easy to follow — no going off on a tangent, talking about the best way to knit a sweater using only a chopstick, a fish knife and a llama called Wilfred. Well, you use the fish...

Structure

Here are some more features of writing to inform and explain. The way you <u>set out</u> your answers can make a <u>big difference</u> to your grade. Pay attention now...

Subheadings *make your work easier to read*

1) Texts like articles can be split up using <u>subheadings</u> — these will help you <u>break up</u> the text, attract the reader's <u>interest</u> and make the article easier to remember.

2) Try to use <u>alliteration</u> (using several words that begin with the same letter) or <u>puns</u> (a play on words) to capture your reader's <u>attention</u>.

| Alliteration Attracts Attention | Rubber, Banned | Seedy Player |

3) Lots of <u>newspaper</u> and <u>magazine</u> articles use these techniques.

Make Connections *within your writing*

As you write, build in some nice <u>linking words</u> to make connections between points. Think about special words and phrases that would help to pull everything together.

> So, now we have looked at activities, let's think about the social side of things. Firstly, the gym is perfect for meeting new people. Not only will you make new friends, it's also great for meeting the opposite sex.

Link *paragraphs together*

<u>Organise</u> your ideas into <u>paragraphs</u>, and make sure they follow a <u>logical order</u>. Most importantly, they need to be <u>linked smoothly</u>. There are special <u>phrases</u> you can use to link paragraphs.

If your writing is <u>formal</u>, use phrases such as:
- Furthermore
- On the other hand
- In contrast

Even <u>informal</u> writing to inform needs to be well <u>organised</u>.

Examiners love these phrases.

If it's <u>informal</u>, you can say things like:
- As I said before
- Later on I realised
- The difference is

Furthermore my dear — I don't give a damn...

Right, so there's another few points that you need to remember when you're busy scribbling in your exam. Don't forget to structure your answer in a sensible way and build up the information and detail when you're explaining something. Simple things, but important.

Techniques

Here are a few more ways of getting those <u>extra marks</u> — try and include some (if not all) of these in your writing. The examiners will just <u>love</u> it.

Use Examples to Support your writing

1) Make sure you <u>back up</u> any points you make with an <u>example</u> or two.

2) Use <u>P.E.E.D.</u> (point, evidence, explanation, development) to <u>explain</u> your examples. This will make your writing more <u>convincing</u>.

3) It's a good idea to use <u>details</u>, <u>quotes</u> and <u>statistics</u> to back up your points. <u>Technical terms</u> will also help you sound knowledgeable.

> Technical terms make it sound like you know what you're talking about.

> The council transports (200 tonnes) of recyclable glass from kerbside collections to the (Materials Recycling Facility) (MRF) every day.

> This sounds much better than "we recycle a lot of glass".

Use some Humour if it's appropriate

Try to use a little <u>humour</u> — especially for a teenage audience, but <u>don't overdo it</u>. The examiners will think that you're a <u>confident writer</u> if you can sometimes use a bit of <u>sarcasm</u> or <u>irony</u> too. Here's a lovely example:

> For the whole of my week in Cornwall, the weather was just delightful — rain every day, howling winds and even, to add to the experience, a raging thunderstorm.

Sue said 'nice shoes' and Trevor thought he'd pulled. He didn't get sarcasm.

Choose your Words carefully

1) Try to use <u>interesting vocabulary</u> — a few <u>sparkling adjectives</u> can liven up a boring passage.

2) Use <u>technical language</u> — but only language your audience will understand. If not, <u>explain</u>.

3) Use <u>similes</u>, e.g. 'The sky <u>was like</u> a sleeping fish.'

4) Use a <u>wide range</u> of techniques, e.g. <u>detail</u>, <u>rhetorical questions</u>, <u>lists</u>, <u>subheadings</u> and <u>personal anecdotes</u> (little stories about your own experiences). This shows off your <u>skills</u> to the examiner.

Use these Phrases in your writing

There are some <u>phrases</u> that can crop up all the time when you're <u>writing to inform</u> or <u>explain</u>. Learn a <u>few</u> so you don't get stuck without any <u>ideas</u> in the exam.

> I would like to inform you of...

> Compare this with the...

> There are many kinds of...

> One of the main points is...

> It is important to...

Humour in an exam — whatever next...

These are all nice little extras that jazz up your writing. They'll make it more interesting and grab you some more marks too. My favourites are anecdotes — especially that one about the pigeon...

Objective and Subjective Writing

Whether you use an objective or subjective style depends on <u>who</u> your writing is aimed at, and <u>why</u> you're writing it — in other words, think about <u>audience</u> and <u>purpose</u>.

Writing can either be Objective or Subjective

1) <u>Objective</u> writing means giving <u>all</u> the main points so that your writing isn't one-sided. E.g.

> A study has shown that 80% of dog owners rated themselves as 'very happy', compared with only 30% of cat owners.

2) <u>Subjective</u> writing means that you're giving your <u>opinion</u>. Subjective statements are generally quite <u>one-sided</u> and only use facts <u>selectively</u> to back up their point of view. E.g.

> Dogs make people happy. It's obvious really — you can't help but feel happy when you're patting a lovely, smiling, friendly dog.

Objective writing has a Neutral Viewpoint

If you were asked to write a letter to your MP explaining how facilities could be improved in your area, for example, you should use an <u>objective style</u> of writing. Here's how:

1) Give a <u>balanced</u> view rather than a one-sided personal opinion.

2) Include plenty of <u>facts</u> and <u>statistics</u> so that your points sound more believable.

3) Try to sound <u>confident</u> so that your writing sounds like the <u>truth</u> rather than just an opinion.

Here are some statistics which are used to back up the points.

> I am writing to you to explain how facilities could be improved in Madeuptown by the proposed funding increase. I help to run the local youth club and we have virtually no money to buy things with. Madeuptown has a large youth population and a high crime rate amongst the under 18s relative to other similar sized towns. Many residents of the town have said that providing these young people with something to do should be a priority. However, senior citizens would also benefit from funding — care homes are currently relying on donations to make ends meet.

These sentences contain opinions, but it's OK — providing differing opinions makes this a balanced, objective piece of writing.

Subjective writing contains the writer's Opinions

1) In your exam, you could be asked to explain your <u>own view</u> on a topic.

2) This is <u>subjective</u> writing — you're giving your own <u>personal opinion</u>. In this sort of writing, it's OK to only mention what <u>you</u> think, and to give a <u>one-sided</u> account. Here's an example:

> I didn't know how much hard work was involved in nursing until I did my work experience. Shifts sometimes started at 5am! The uniform was a bit dull, but I wore it anyway.

Here's a personal opinion — this is subjective.

I'd be being subjective if I said this page wasn't easy...

I know it's tricky at first, but make sure you know the difference between objective and subjective writing. Have a go at finding some examples around your home — e.g. look in newspapers and leaflets — and try working out whether the author is being subjective or objective.

Writing Your Own

By now you should have the <u>theory</u> sorted, so it's time to put it all into <u>practice</u>.

Look out for these Examples of Writing to Inform or Explain

In your exam, you could get asked to write any of the following:

1) A Newspaper or Magazine Article

Write an article for a local newspaper, explaining an issue that is causing concern.

→ You're <u>informing</u> people about something that's been happening.

Here's a possible introduction:

Interesting language →

Local residents are appealing against the council's decision to allow a (notorious) music festival to go ahead in the fields that back onto their houses. (Bands from all over Europe are expected to descend on Littleton) and (residents fear the huge crowds will cause havoc.)

Mix of fact and opinion

Briefly cover all the <u>main points</u> in the <u>introduction</u>.

2) An Account of an Event

Write an account informing the reader of a memorable event from your childhood.

→ This type of writing is more <u>personal</u>.

Here's an extract from a student's answer:

Susie's passport photo...

(My earliest memory) is of going on holiday with my younger sister, Susie. I remember my overwhelming fear of the planes — they were like (giant birds swooping out of the sky.) Susie took it all in her stride; I suppose she was too young to really know (what was going on.)

...never did improve.

Interesting detail

You can organise your account <u>chronologically</u> (in the order that it happened) but it's often more interesting if you don't.

Less formal language

3) A Letter

Write a letter to your local MP inviting them to attend a school debate. Explain all the necessary details.

→ This letter should be <u>formal</u> because it's to an MP.

Here's an extract from an example answer:

Formal, factual language →

(We are holding a debate on the subject of whether) it is the responsibility of the Government to combat the increasing incidence of childhood obesity. We would like to invite you to attend as a representative of the Government. The debate will be held at (10.15am on Monday 22nd September.)

Clear information, clearly organised

Who? What? Why? Enough with the questions...

When you spot a question asking you to inform or explain, try to work out who the audience is, what form you'll need to write in and what you need to tell them about. Armed with these tasty morsels you'll be able to choose your tone and style of language to fit, and get loads of marks.

Writing Your Own

The exam board may have <u>other forms</u> up their sleeve, but if you've <u>practised</u> all of these you'll be <u>prepared</u> for anything. Oh, except fire eating of course — you'd better not try that just yet.

Don't forget these Types of Writing to Inform or Explain

4) A Leaflet

Write an information leaflet for a tourist attraction in your area.

An information leaflet can be <u>formal or informal</u>, <u>serious or entertaining</u>. The key is <u>organisation</u>.

Here's an extract from a student's answer:

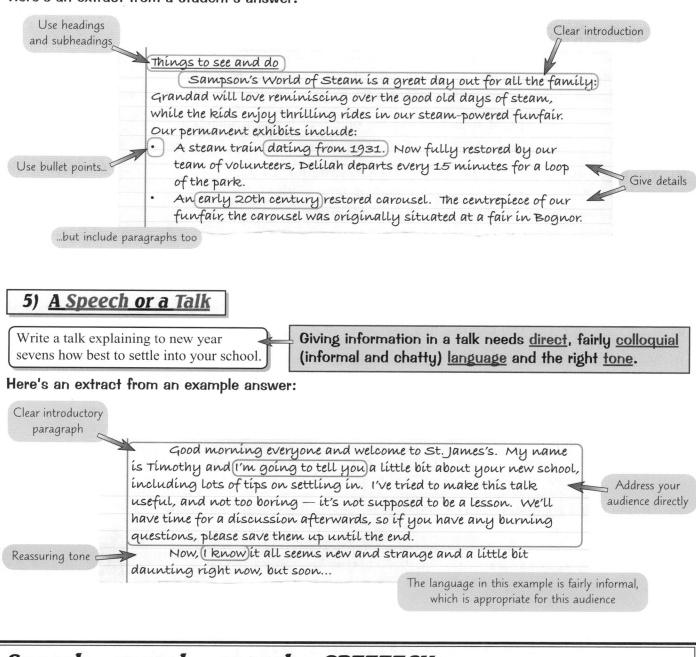

Use headings and subheadings

Clear introduction

Things to see and do

Sampson's World of Steam is a great day out for all the family: Grandad will love reminiscing over the good old days of steam, while the kids enjoy thrilling rides in our steam-powered funfair. Our permanent exhibits include:

Use bullet points...

- A steam train dating from 1931. Now fully restored by our team of volunteers, Delilah departs every 15 minutes for a loop of the park.
- An early 20th century restored carousel. The centrepiece of our funfair, the carousel was originally situated at a fair in Bognor.

Give details

...but include paragraphs too

5) A Speech or a Talk

Write a talk explaining to new year sevens how best to settle into your school.

Giving information in a talk needs <u>direct</u>, fairly <u>colloquial</u> (informal and chatty) <u>language</u> and the right <u>tone</u>.

Here's an extract from an example answer:

Clear introductory paragraph

Good morning everyone and welcome to St. James's. My name is Timothy and I'm going to tell you a little bit about your new school, including lots of tips on settling in. I've tried to make this talk useful, and not too boring — it's not supposed to be a lesson. We'll have time for a discussion afterwards, so if you have any burning questions, please save them up until the end.

Address your audience directly

Reassuring tone

Now, I know it all seems new and strange and a little bit daunting right now, but soon...

The language in this example is fairly informal, which is appropriate for this audience

Speech... speech... speech... SPEEEECH...

When you're writing to inform or explain, work out which pieces of information are important, and which should be left out to avoid bamboozling your audience. Plan ahead — it's the only way.

Writing to Describe

One of the types of writing you might be lucky enough to do in your <u>exam</u> or <u>controlled assessment</u> is "<u>writing to describe</u>". Here are some of the things you should bear in mind when you get to it...

You're painting a Picture with Words

1) When you're <u>writing to describe</u>, you need to remember that the <u>reader</u> won't have exactly the same <u>picture</u> in their head as you have in yours — you need to <u>draw it</u> for them with words.

2) This means being as <u>expressive</u> as you can, and coming up with <u>inventive</u> ways to describe whatever it is you're thinking about.

Think about your Purpose and Audience

1) Your purpose is to <u>describe</u> — simple as that. You might be asked to "describe an object or place that means a lot to you" for example. So think about:

> • <u>what</u> it is that makes the object or place meaningful
> • <u>how</u> you can describe those things in detail

2) You might not be given a specific <u>audience</u> to write for, so just imagine you're writing for the person <u>marking</u> your work.

3) Try and base your answers on your <u>own experiences</u>.

Imagine you're making a Film of the scene

If you're writing about a <u>place</u>, try to imagine that you're making a <u>film</u> of your scene, and describing what will happen in it. You can use this technique to give your writing some <u>structure</u>.

1) You could think about how the scene will <u>look</u> at <u>different times</u> of the day, or in <u>different seasons</u> of the year. You can use this to show a <u>contrast</u> in atmosphere.

> The beach was a desolate grey plain, devoid of all life and movement apart from the soft splosh of waves as they calmly rearranged every pebble and stone they fell on. It was hard to believe that in less than a month the beach would be the vibrant focal point of the summer, alive with tourists and deck chairs.

2) Or you could <u>zoom</u> in or out of your scene, <u>describing things</u> as you go.

> I was only feet away from the last of the day's fishermen, still standing vigil on the ochre waters. The reflections of trees shimmered on the surface, and in the distance I could just make out the hazy form of hills.

Oh daarling, I'm simply overcome with all this loveliness...

OK so all this "paint a picture with words" stuff might sound a bit namby pamby, but it really is the best way to get this right. Just make sure you plan before you write — write down all your ideas in a plan, then when everything's in front of you, you can put it into a good order.

Writing to Describe

Writing to describe isn't <u>just</u> about giving the reader a picture of something in words.
The best writers will use who or what they're describing to actually reflect <u>thoughts</u> and <u>feelings</u>.

Don't just state the Obvious

If you want to tell the reader how you <u>feel</u> about the thing you're
describing, don't just write "I am frightened" or "I am happy" or whatever.
Instead, use <u>imagery</u> to help the reader understand your <u>emotions</u>.

Imagine you're asked to "describe the room you are in". Rather than just giving the colours of
the walls and describing the furniture, try to <u>express emotions</u> through your description, like so:

> Even the walls appear to be bulging with
> the pressure of the panic within them.

The panic the writer feels has been
emphasised by talking about it as if
it's physical — something that's solid
enough to put pressure on a wall.

Think about the Viewpoint you're going to write from

1) The <u>viewpoint</u> you write from can make your description more <u>interesting</u>.

2) If you're asked to write a description of a <u>zoo</u>, the way you describe it will
   be different depending on whether it's from <u>your viewpoint</u> or a <u>penguin's</u>:

   - If you write as a visitor, you may want to create a sense of <u>fun</u> or <u>curiosity</u>.
   - If you choose to write as a penguin, you could create a sense of
     <u>tedious boredom</u> — another <u>forgettable</u> hour of being watched.

Use the Senses to improve your Description

1) Try and use the senses of <u>sound</u>, <u>sight</u> and <u>smell</u> in your description:

> All that could be heard was the rustling of autumn leaves as
> they were gently stirred by the wind. A cloth of darkness
> made it impossible to make out the advancing shapes, as the
> acrid stench of rotten meat assailed our nostrils.

sound — sight — smell

2) For an even better description,
   you could also have a go at
   using <u>touch</u> and <u>taste</u>:

> The walls were slimy and cool beneath my probing
> fingers, as the bitterness of bile rose to my mouth.

touch — taste

3) When you describe using the senses, don't go for the obvious. Instead of "the sea was blue with
   white waves", you could write "the sea was a <u>shimmering azure</u> with <u>vanilla foam-flecked</u> waves".

Panic? Tedious boredom? Rotten meat? Not in this book.

It really is worth taking a few extra seconds to come up with an unusual way of describing things
— you can make fairly straightforward stuff sound much more interesting. Right, I'm off to buy a
comforting vessel of smouldering dark gold with a vanilla foam-flecked head. Or maybe just a coffee.

Imagery

Good writers often use <u>imagery</u> to develop their writing — imagery creates a picture in the reader's mind. <u>Similes</u>, <u>metaphors</u> and <u>personification</u> are all types of imagery you might fancy using.

Use Imagery to develop your descriptions

<u>Similes</u>, <u>metaphors</u> and <u>personification</u> are comparisons — they compare one thing to another. They're really useful for spicing up your descriptions.

> <u>Similes</u> describe something by saying that it is <u>like</u> something else. They usually use the words "<u>as</u>" or "<u>like</u>". For example:
>
> > "The echo of the sea pounding in the caverns is <u>like</u> the thud of a mother's heartbeat to the baby in her womb."

> <u>Metaphors</u> describe something by saying that it <u>is</u> something else. For example:
>
> > "The night <u>was</u> a warm, damp blanket muffling the sound of traffic."

> <u>Personification</u> is where a <u>non-living object</u> is given <u>human</u> or <u>animal features</u>. Like this:
>
> > "The wind was a wolf, howling through the alleyways."

There's also alliteration here ("<u>w</u>ind <u>w</u>as a <u>w</u>olf") to create a sound effect of the wind.

This example is also a metaphor.

There's onomatopoeia too — "howling" imitates the noise of the wind to help create the sound in the reader's mind.

parp

I think that's a typo — it should say 'the wolf had wind'.

Use Imagery like this...

Using <u>imagery</u> in your writing really adds <u>expression</u> and makes the whole thing much more <u>interesting</u>. Have a look at this description of an exam hall...

The storm metaphor shows the writer's anxiety.

We are worryingly adrift in a storm of deep-blue floor-tiles. The hands of the clock are speeding up: they wait for me to glance away and then sail swiftly to their next port of call. No safe harbour is in sight.

The personification of the clock's hands emphasises the feeling of panic and lack of time.

The sea metaphor from before is brought up again here. It adds to the feeling of insecurity.

This page is a rapturous burst of burnished sunshine...

Well OK, maybe not, but it's pretty important stuff so make sure you've got the hang of using imagery, and that you know the difference between similes, metaphors and personification.

Techniques

To keep your writing <u>interesting</u> (and to bag yourself some <u>big marks</u>), it's a good idea to vary the <u>length</u> and <u>structure</u> of your <u>sentences</u>. So read on...

Short Sentences increase the Pace...

To make part of your description sound fast-moving and exciting, <u>shorten</u> your sentences.
To make part of your description sound thoughtful and sophisticated, <u>lengthen</u> your sentences.

It's freezing out here.
Sandals were a bad choice.

SHORT: The sky darkened to leaden grey. Heavy rain hammered on my roof. The urge to scream was unbearable.

LONG: The remnants of the morning mist crouched over the fields, a low-lying cloud, swirling and evaporating as my sandalled feet drifted through it.

Use Compound and Complex Sentences like this...

<u>Simple</u> sentences can be effective but don't use too many of them.
Use <u>compound</u> and <u>complex</u> sentences to keep your writing interesting and varied.

Simple sentence
We crept soundlessly outside. The darkness engulfed us.

Compound sentence
We crept soundlessly outside and the darkness engulfed us.

The sentences are joined with "and" or "or" to make a compound sentence.

Complex sentence
We crept soundlessly outside, despite the engulfing darkness.

Now the two points are separated by a comma.

Young Timothy was sent home early for failing to include a complex sentence in his piece of prose. Fool.

Repeat Words or Short Phrases for effect

<u>Repeating</u> words or short phrases is a good way of emphasising your key points and making them more <u>memorable</u> for the reader.
Repeating words <u>three times</u> ('the rule of three') is especially effective.

The repetition of the word 'flame' really drums in the sense of intense heat and light from the setting sun.

In Crete, the setting sun is a flame. A blazing flame. A shimmering flame which spills its fire onto the ocean, like a blacksmith raking his coals.

Remember to use metaphors and similes, but don't overdo it.

I never repeat myself, I never repeat myself, no never...

Remember to use as many interesting verbs, adjectives and adverbs as you can. If you can show off some vocabulary then the markers will be ecstatic. Well, fairly pleased. So instead of saying things like "walk quickly", you could use "scurry frantically", or "stride purposefully". Easy peasy...

Writing Your Own

Here are some more <u>practical tips</u> on answering the question.

It's usually 'Describe a Place' or 'Describe a Person'

1) You'll normally be asked to talk about a <u>place</u> or <u>person</u>. Questions asking you to <u>describe</u> are often quite <u>open-ended</u>, so you can approach them in different ways.

2) The idea is that you're <u>not limited</u> — you've got the chance to be really <u>imaginative</u> and <u>creative</u>.

3) So it's a really good idea to write all of your ideas down in a <u>plan</u> before you set off.

4) If you were asked to describe a <u>terrifying place</u>, for example, you could get <u>ideas</u> from anywhere:

> paintings   music lyrics   First day at school   sci-fi films
>
> medieval dungeons   prison   natural disasters   being trapped   war

Develop your ideas using Spider Diagrams

You could draw a <u>spider diagram</u> as your plan to get some ideas flowing.

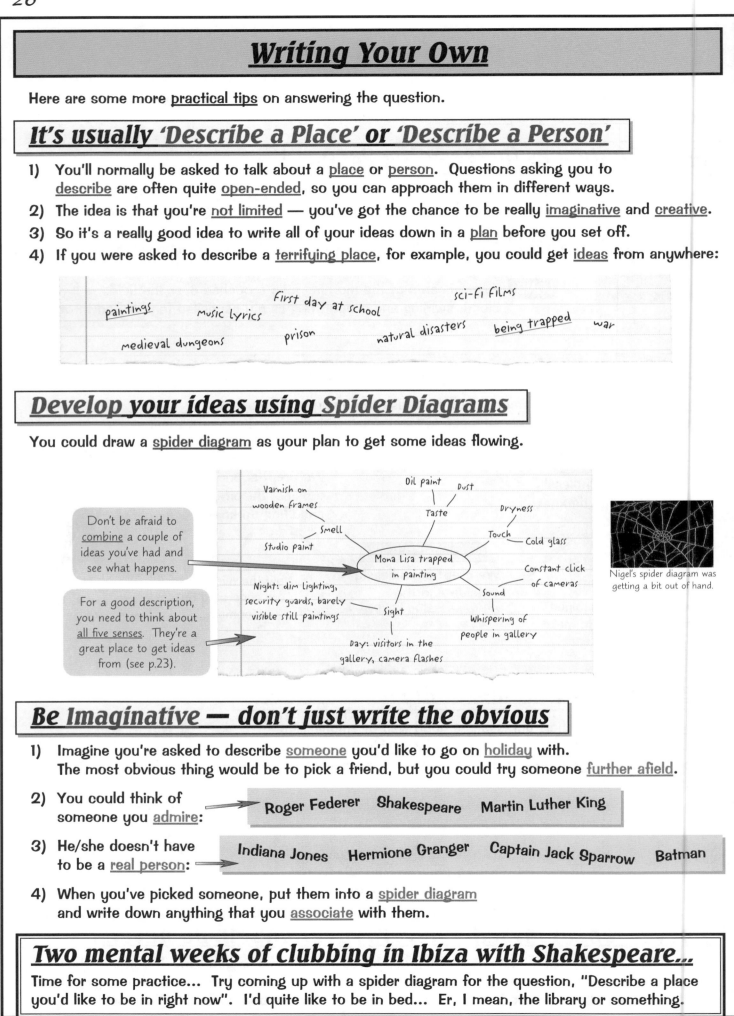

Don't be afraid to <u>combine</u> a couple of ideas you've had and see what happens.

For a good description, you need to think about <u>all five senses</u>. They're a great place to get ideas from (see p.23).

Varnish on wooden frames
Oil paint   Dust
Taste   Dryness
Smell   Touch   Cold glass
Studio paint
Mona Lisa trapped in painting   Constant click of cameras
Night: dim lighting, security guards, barely visible still paintings   Sound
Sight   Whispering of people in gallery
Day: visitors in the gallery, camera flashes

Nigel's spider diagram was getting a bit out of hand.

Be Imaginative — don't just write the obvious

1) Imagine you're asked to describe <u>someone</u> you'd like to go on <u>holiday</u> with. The most obvious thing would be to pick a friend, but you could try someone <u>further afield</u>.

2) You could think of someone you <u>admire</u>:   Roger Federer   Shakespeare   Martin Luther King

3) He/she doesn't have to be a <u>real person</u>:   Indiana Jones   Hermione Granger   Captain Jack Sparrow   Batman

4) When you've picked someone, put them into a <u>spider diagram</u> and write down anything that you <u>associate</u> with them.

Two mental weeks of clubbing in Ibiza with Shakespeare...

Time for some practice... Try coming up with a spider diagram for the question, "Describe a place you'd like to be in right now". I'd quite like to be in bed... Er, I mean, the library or something.

Writing Your Own

Your writing needs three sections — a <u>start</u>, a <u>finish</u> and a well-structured <u>middle bit</u>.
You need to think about how best to keep the reader <u>interested</u> through all three parts.

Use your Opening to grab the reader's Attention

Your <u>first sentence</u> has to let the reader know what you're
<u>writing about</u>, but more importantly, make them want to <u>read on</u>.

For example, for the '<u>terrifying place</u>' answer on the previous
page, your first sentence could be something <u>like this</u>:

> There's some interesting vocabulary here to get the reader's attention.

> Immediately talking as if you're the Mona Lisa is an unusual idea that might intrigue the reader.

> My (enigmatic) smile is still as fresh as the day it was painted, politely (concealing) five hundred years of (boredom) and (frustration.)

> It's clear how she feels about being trapped in a painting right from the beginning.

In the Middle, try using an Interesting Structure

1) Once you've captivated your readers with your intro, you'll need to <u>develop</u> your <u>ideas</u>.

2) If you've <u>planned</u> your work properly before starting writing, you'll already have your ideas in a <u>logical order</u>. For <u>extra marks</u> though, have a go at an <u>unusual</u> structure.

3) Look at how a <u>countdown</u> of minutes has been used to build up the <u>atmosphere</u> here:

> Ten minutes to go, and the walls appear to be shifting inwards of their own accord.
> Five minutes left, and I can hear the enemy preparing their weapons on the other side of the wall.
> Two minutes; were this a space mission they would be beginning the countdown.

At the End, you can go Back to the Start...

You should <u>plan your ending</u>. One idea for a good ending is to come back to the way you <u>started</u>. Here's an ending to go with the Mona Lisa story at the top of the page.

> So now I'm here, my once smooth lips chapped with age but still forced into that mystifying smile, destined to live in my cold, sterile world forever.

> The tension's built up right until the end.

...or reveal some Withheld Information

Another good idea is to have a <u>surprise ending</u>... (this isn't for the Mona Lisa story).

> A short sentence in between long ones adds to the tension.

> I thought I had been reprieved and began to plan my swift but silent exit. (Suddenly the door was flung wide open.) The masked figure filled the doorway, blocking from view the instruments of torture beyond, as her strident tones echoed around the chamber, ("Mr Jones, the dentist will see you now".)

> Surprise!

ELEPHANT DUNG PYJAMAS — that got your attention...

Remember, you don't necessarily have to write a story. You'll get top marks for writing imaginatively, structuring your work carefully and using good vocab, whether it's fictional or not.

Writing to Argue and Persuade

Now you're going to learn how to <u>argue</u> and <u>persuade</u>. No, no, put your fists (and your money) away — it's not about fighting or bribery. It's about <u>putting across</u> your <u>point of view</u> successfully.

Here's what you'll get in the Exam

1) In section B of your Unit 1 exam, you have to answer <u>two questions</u>.
2) One of these questions will ask you to <u>argue</u>, <u>persuade</u> or <u>advise</u>.
3) Arguments can be written in different forms, e.g. <u>letters</u>, <u>reports</u>, <u>speeches</u> and <u>articles</u>.

Writing an argument Doesn't mean getting Angry

Writing to argue <u>doesn't</u> mean having a good old angry rant at the examiner. What it <u>does</u> mean is putting across your <u>point of view</u> about a topic.

It's also important to show that you've considered <u>alternative</u> points of view. You do this by describing the other points of view, and then explaining why they're wrong. This is called using <u>counter-arguments</u>.

See page 33 for more about using counter-arguments.

Persuasive writing tries to Change Opinions

Here are examples of persuasive writing that you could be asked to write in the exam:

1) A persuasive Letter

You could be asked to write a letter to a <u>newspaper</u> or to an <u>important person</u> like an MP to try and change their opinion about an issue. Like so:

Emotive language emphasises how important this complaint is.

I was (appalled) to find that despite several complaints to the council, there are still no street lamps on Parkway Common. Something must be done (urgently.)

This encourages the reader to take action quickly.

2) A persuasive Speech

When writing a persuasive speech, it's important to think about how the words will <u>sound</u> when they're read out.

Repeating the 'u' sound here is an example of alliteration. It sounds great read out loud.

"Ladies and Gentlemen, we are here today to listen to the cases (for and against) the ugly, unfashionable and upsetting trend that is school uniform."

Look — it's presented as balanced equal debate...

...even though it clearly isn't. The speaker's opinions are obvious from the start.

Make me a cup of tea and I'll be your best friend...

It can be a bit tricky to get your point across whilst also showing that you understand alternative viewpoints. Try not to resort to name-calling, hair-pulling and other generalised insults.

Writing to Argue and Persuade

The way you write to argue or persuade depends a lot on your <u>audience</u> — you'd use <u>different</u> <u>language</u> if you were writing for your <u>headteacher</u> than if you were writing for your <u>best friend</u>.

Think about the Purpose, Form and Audience

Writing to argue or persuade usually involves writing in a particular <u>form</u> — things like <u>articles</u>, <u>speeches</u> and <u>letters</u> are always a safe bet. You'll also have to write with different <u>audiences</u> in mind.

1) The first thing you should do is read the <u>question</u> carefully.

2) Then jot down the <u>purpose</u>, <u>form</u> and <u>audience</u> for the question.

3) The question will usually <u>tell</u> you who the audience is. If it doesn't, then write your answer for the <u>examiner</u>.

4) Also check whether you've been asked to argue or persuade <u>for</u> something, <u>against</u> something, or whether you can <u>decide</u> this for yourself.

Some Forms have a Specific Audience

You might be told <u>who</u> to <u>aim</u> your argument at — e.g. <u>teenage girls</u>, <u>cyclists</u>, <u>bird watchers</u> etc. This is your <u>audience</u>. Here's an example:

> Write an article for a magazine aimed at teenagers in which you argue that students should be taught to drive at school.

Purpose = argue
Form = magazine article
Audience = teenagers

It's important to think about your <u>audience</u>, as this will affect the <u>tone</u> of your writing. For example, if your audience is someone older and/or in a position of authority then you will need to show that you can write in a <u>formal</u> tone.

If you're writing an article for students, you can use a more <u>relaxed tone</u> and more <u>colloquial language</u>.

Recently, a number of incidents have occurred outside the leisure centre...

Look at how formal this language is.

This language is quite colloquial.

You'll get a real buzz the first time you sit in the driver's seat.

Adverts try to Persuade you to Buy something

<u>Adverts</u> are really obvious examples of persuasive writing. Their purpose is to persuade you that their product is the best.

New Sparkly Brite washing powder leaves your whites 50% brighter than the leading brand. It's the freshest smelling too. Mmm.

Facts and figures help back up any points, but they are likely to be opinion too.

This is only an opinion, but it's presented like a fact.

I'd rather do GCSE driving than GCSE English...

There are many other types of persuasive writing that you could be asked to use — you might have to persuade <u>tourists</u> to visit your town or persuade <u>parents</u> that your school is great.

Structure and Techniques

There are a number of <u>techniques</u> you can use to get good <u>marks</u> in this paper.
When you're writing to argue you need to include a few of these to impress the examiner.

Here's a list of Techniques you can use to argue

On this page and the next three, you'll find stuff about all these different techniques:

emotive language	facts and statistics	quoting authorities	generalisations
rhetorical questions	counter-arguments	flattery	personal anecdotes
irony and satire	different tenses	repetition	exaggerations

Use Emotive Language to get through to your reader

1) Emotive language is language that provokes an <u>emotional reaction</u> in the reader, like anger, disgust or sadness.

2) You could tell them some <u>shocking</u> or <u>disturbing</u> facts, for example.

> An increasing number of young people are (tragically killed) or left permanently (disabled) and (disfigured) due to reckless driving.

3) You could also use <u>contrasting adjectives</u>. In this description, the adjectives are used to provoke an <u>emotional response</u>. The reader will feel <u>sorry</u> for the rabbits and so will be encouraged to take the view that the scientists are <u>evil</u>.

> Strong adjectives encourage the reader to see things in a certain light.

> These (vile) scientists use (innocent, friendly and helpless) rabbits in their experiments. The unfortunate creatures might otherwise be loved by a child in a kind home.

> These three words build up a picture of the rabbit as a victim. Using three words together for effect is called 'the rule of three'.

Flattery gets you everywhere

1) A great way to persuade is to <u>flatter</u> your <u>readers</u>. If you <u>compliment</u> them, they'll think you have good taste and will be more likely to agree with you on your other points. Clever...

2) Tell them how much you <u>value</u> them or that you know how <u>intelligent</u> they are. That sort of thing.

3) Also flatter the <u>product</u> or <u>idea</u> that you're trying to advertise. You can do this using "<u>superlatives</u>" — phrases that use the word "<u>most</u>" or words that have -<u>est</u> at the end of the word, (e.g. "the fastest, most dazzling horse").

Mr Jones had spent so much in the tackle shop that he was in with a chance of winning some worms.

In the letter below, the reader is told that they are very <u>important</u> and the prize draw is made to sound <u>great</u>.

> Dear Mr Jones, you are one of our (most highly valued) customers and for this reason you have been specially selected to take part in a (once-in-a-lifetime) prize draw.

> This flatters the reader and makes him feel special.

> The prize draw is made to sound really exciting and unmissable.

If flattery gets you everywhere, why do we use cars?

It might seem obvious, but if you're nice to people, they become more receptive to your point of view. So writing positively and giving a few compliments will mean they are more likely to listen if you try to persuade them to change something or do something. It's a clever trick to remember.

Structure and Techniques

Here are some more. Concentrate now.

Use Facts and Statistics to prove your point

1) Aim to include some <u>facts</u> and <u>statistics</u> in your writing.

2) You can <u>make these up</u> if you like, but make sure they sound <u>realistic</u>.

3) They'll make your argument more <u>convincing</u>.

> 70% of students agree that, by wearing a school uniform, they are less likely to behave badly on their way to and from school.

4) <u>Facts</u> are true. <u>Opinions</u> are what someone <u>believes</u> to be true, even if they're not. A great way to make your writing persuasive is by presenting your <u>opinions as facts</u> (this is called "<u>assertion</u>").

This makes it sound true even though it's an opinion.

> It is obvious that this is a brilliant school and it is clear that everyone who attends it will do very well.

This phrase also makes the opinion sound like a fact.

Quote Authorities to convince your audience

1) You can make your argument sound even more <u>convincing</u> if you <u>quote</u> people who would be expected to know about the subject.

2) You could quote doctors, scientists, politicians etc.

3) Again, you can make these up — just make sure they sound <u>believable</u>.

> Scientists at NASA have recently proved that the human body is not designed to stand still for more than 7 minutes at a time. During assembly we are frequently forced to stand for over 20 minutes....

Add Generalisations to sound more convincing

1) Generalisations are <u>sweeping statements</u> about a subject.

2) They're a good way to sound <u>forceful</u> and <u>convincing</u>.

> Most of the students at this school feel that wearing ties in the summer is pointless.

Include Personal Anecdotes to add interest

To make your writing <u>personal</u>, aim to include an <u>anecdote</u> — a little story relevant to your argument which involves <u>you</u> or another person. It'll <u>back up</u> your points and show the reader that you know what you're talking about.

> When I first came to school I was shocked to find that there was nowhere to get a drink of water during the day. I remember how thirsty I felt.

Personal anecdotes show you have experience of the topic in question.

83% of students skipped right past this page...

English isn't too bad really — there aren't many subjects where your teacher would tell you to make up facts, statistics and quotes in the exam. Shame you can't do it with Geography.

Structure and Techniques

Righty-ho. On this page we have some of the most <u>incredible</u> stuff you'll <u>ever</u> learn in your life and we discuss why ants can't look left. OK, OK, I'm exaggerating — but it's just as interesting.

Exaggeration can give your ideas loads more Oomph

1) Writers use <u>exaggeration</u> to make points seem more <u>important</u> to the reader.

2) This is very <u>effective</u> in persuasive writing. If there is a <u>problem</u> with something, say there is a <u>huge problem</u> with it. If you think something is <u>bad</u>, say you are <u>appalled and disgusted</u> by it.

3) It's <u>not lying</u> as such — just <u>bending the truth</u>. Here's an example:

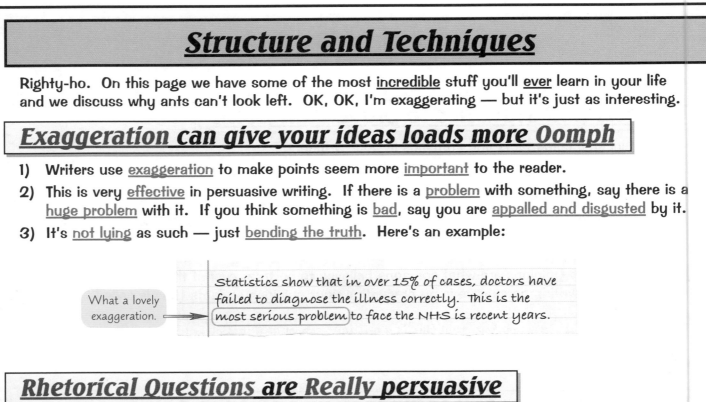

What a lovely exaggeration. →

Statistics show that in over 15% of cases, doctors have failed to diagnose the illness correctly. This is the most serious problem to face the NHS is recent years.

Rhetorical Questions are Really persuasive

Rhetorical questions are questions that <u>don't need an answer</u>. They're usually <u>leading</u> <u>questions</u> which encourage the audience to agree with the writer's opinion. They're a really effective way to <u>start</u> a persuasive essay. Here are some examples:

Does this child need to die of malnutrition?

Don't you think it's time we saw an end to war?

Are you ready for the greatest product you have ever seen?

<u>Rhetorical questions</u> are also a really good way to <u>end</u> an argument — they <u>remind</u> the readers what the issue is all about, and persuade them to change their <u>point of view</u>.

Use Irony and Satire to ridicule alternative arguments

1) Use humour very <u>carefully</u>. It has to be <u>clever</u> and not rude or silly. One of the best ways to use humour in your argument is to use <u>irony</u> or <u>satire</u>.

2) <u>Irony</u> is when the <u>literal</u> meaning and the <u>intended</u> meaning of your words are the <u>opposite</u> of each other. It's a clever way of making your argument funny.

3) <u>Satire</u> is usually written in quite a <u>serious tone</u>, so that at first your reader thinks what you're saying should be taken seriously. Once they read on, they begin to realise that there is an intentional different <u>meaning</u>.

4) You can use satire to make alternative points of view appear <u>ridiculous</u>.

Of course all students should be made to wear ties, jumpers and blazers in the middle of summer. This would help the government achieve its targets on cutting childhood obesity. Students wearing full uniform during a heatwave lose, I would estimate, about 3lb per day.

Don't you just hate rhetorical questions?

It may be difficult to come up with a good-un, but a well thought out rhetorical question can work wonders when put in the right place. It gets people involved in the topic.

Structure and Techniques

Just one more page on techniques — these are a few more ways to really
<u>strengthen</u> your <u>argument</u> and <u>persuade</u> the audience to <u>agree</u> with you.

Use Counter-Arguments to present alternative ideas

Writing to argue is all about giving opinions, but remember to include some opinions which
go <u>against</u> your argument ('<u>counter-arguments</u>'). If you're clever, you can use these
counter-arguments to show how much stronger <u>your</u> argument is. Here's an example:

> You should include opinions which are different from yours...

70% of teachers claim that driving lessons aren't as important as the regular curriculum. However, their argument centres on the fact that they wouldn't have enough time to cover the curriculum if driving lessons were introduced. By providing driving lessons after school or during lunch times, lesson time would be unaffected, but students would still have the benefit of learning to drive in the safety of school.

> ...but then you can go on to show the strength of your argument.

Use Different Tenses to build up your points

1) Using different <u>tenses</u> is quite an effective way of <u>building up</u> your points.

2) Start in the <u>past</u> tense, move to the <u>present</u> and then you can even
    speculate on the <u>future</u> if you fancy.

I used to share this opinion on the importance of homework. Now I believe that too many teachers are setting homework with no clear purpose. In the next few weeks I think that the school should review the homework policy.

"...homework makes me travel sick when I copy it off my friend on the bus to school..."

Use Repetition to emphasise key points

1) You can <u>repeat</u> words or short phrases to <u>emphasise</u> your key points.

2) In particular, repeating things <u>three times</u> is a clever <u>trick</u>
    that will help your reader to <u>remember</u> your points.

It's outrageous to suggest that pupils don't work hard. It's outrageous to suggest that we are all lazy good-for-nothings. And it's especially outrageous to expect us to take on even more homework.

Some people don't follow my advice... However...

Aren't counter-arguments fun? I like them. You get to sound all clever and articulate, but all you're
doing is going on about how everyone else is wrong and how you're right. I could do that all day.

Writing Your Own

When you're writing to <u>persuade</u> or <u>argue</u>, it's important to think about the <u>structure</u>. You're more likely to <u>convince</u> your audience if you present a <u>well-structured</u> case.

Persuasive writing and arguments need Structure

You need to ensure that you get your point across in the most <u>clear</u>, <u>concise</u> and <u>effective</u> way. Here's a good way to do it:

1) <u>Introduction</u> — set out the <u>main topic</u>.
2) <u>Early development</u> — <u>build</u> on the opening statements.
3) <u>Later development</u> — suggest what you want readers to <u>do</u> and <u>why</u>.
4) <u>Conclusion</u> — strong <u>final</u> section to <u>reinforce</u> the main points.

Don't think this means you have to stick to four paragraphs. Use as many paragraphs as you like.

Remember these Two Important Points

Imagine you've got a question asking you to write to your headteacher persuading him or her to get rid of school uniform. Now's your chance to be really, you know, <u>persuasive</u>. Don't forget to read the question carefully and write down a <u>plan</u> before you start.

1) Think about your Audience

The <u>audience</u> you're writing for is really important. Who your audience is will determine what <u>style</u> you need to write in. For example, you should be <u>formal</u> when you're writing to your headteacher:

Dear Mrs Hughes
I am writing to express my concerns about our school's uniform.

2) Express yourself Clearly

Once you have written a <u>clear introduction</u>, you need to:

1) <u>Build up</u> the <u>detail</u> by writing down all the <u>specific points</u>.
2) Make sure you write every separate point <u>clearly</u> and <u>fully</u>.

Don't throw all your points at them at once.

Use evidence to add weight to your point.

Good list of adjectives and the 'rule of three'.

Year after year, we have worn the same tasteless, dull and uncomfortable uniform. It is expensive to buy, £159 altogether, and does not show our school to be the forward-thinking institution that it is.

This will get the headteacher to think about others people's opinions — a good tactic.

If you can't persuade them, just SHOUT LOUDER...

Well, this may work on your sister, but it's not always the best way to go about things. Try to understand how people may feel about things, and base your persuasive attack around their views.

Writing Your Own

The techniques you use can make <u>all the difference</u>. Don't worry, I won't leave you hanging...

Decide on your Argument

1) In this question, you need to <u>decide</u> whether you are going to argue <u>for</u> or <u>against</u> being taught to drive in school.

2) Jot down a few points which are both <u>for</u> or <u>against</u> your argument.

3) Then decide which <u>points</u> to include and in which <u>order</u>.

4) If you decide to argue <u>against</u>, you can still use the points <u>for</u> as counter-arguments, e.g.

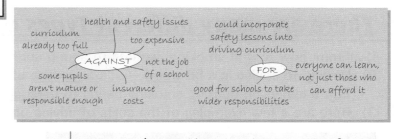

health and safety issues
curriculum already too full
too expensive
AGAINST
not the job of a school
some pupils aren't mature or responsible enough
insurance costs

could incorporate safety lessons into driving curriculum
FOR
everyone can learn, not just those who can afford it
good for schools to take wider responsibilities

Although it could be argued that road safety lessons could be incorporated into the driving curriculum, some pupils would still lack the maturity to drive in a responsible manner.

Use a Variety of Persuasive Techniques

Here's a <u>letter</u> trying to persuade a town council not to open a new out-of-town supermarket. There are loads of different <u>persuasive writing</u> techniques in it.

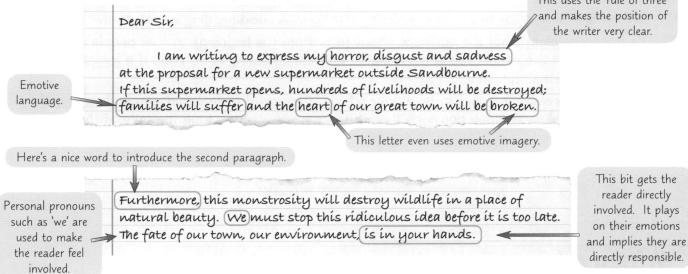

Dear Sir,

I am writing to express my <u>horror, disgust and sadness</u> at the proposal for a new supermarket outside Sandbourne. If this supermarket opens, hundreds of livelihoods will be destroyed; <u>families will suffer</u> and the <u>heart</u> of our great town will be <u>broken.</u>

This uses the 'rule of three' and makes the position of the writer very clear.

Emotive language.

This letter even uses emotive imagery.

Here's a nice word to introduce the second paragraph.

Personal pronouns such as 'we' are used to make the reader feel involved.

<u>Furthermore,</u> this monstrosity will destroy wildlife in a place of natural beauty. <u>We</u> must stop this ridiculous idea before it is too late. The fate of our town, our environment, <u>is in your hands.</u>

This bit gets the reader directly involved. It plays on their emotions and implies they are directly responsible.

Don't forget to include some of the <u>techniques</u> covered on the previous pages. You could include <u>repetition</u>, <u>statistics</u>, <u>quoting authorities</u> etc. Here's the driving lesson example developed using a few more:

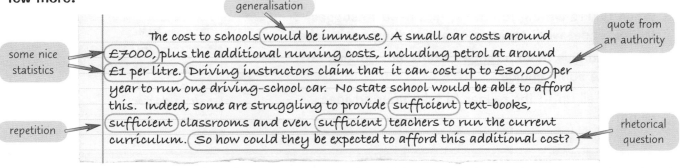

generalisation

some nice statistics

repetition

The cost to schools <u>would be immense.</u> A small car costs around <u>£7000,</u> plus the additional running costs, including petrol at around <u>£1 per litre.</u> <u>Driving instructors claim that it can cost up to £30,000</u> per year to run one driving-school car. No state school would be able to afford this. Indeed, some are struggling to provide <u>sufficient</u> text-books, <u>sufficient</u> classrooms and even <u>sufficient</u> teachers to run the current curriculum. <u>So how could they be expected to afford this additional cost?</u>

quote from an authority

rhetorical question

Blackmail is not a persuasive technique...

There's a lot of information crammed into the last few pages, but don't worry, that's it for this section.

Writing to Advise

When you're writing to <u>advise</u>, you want to <u>help</u> the reader. You need to get them on your side so that they're prepared to pay attention to your gems of wisdom.

There are many different Types of advice

1) From 'how to quit smoking' leaflets to agony aunt pages, written advice is <u>everywhere</u>.

2) Writing to advise is a bit <u>weird</u> — it's a <u>mixture</u> of writing to <u>inform</u> and writing to <u>persuade</u>.
   E.g. a leaflet on quitting smoking needs to <u>persuade</u> people to <u>quit</u> and <u>inform</u> them <u>how</u> to do it.

3) Here are a few <u>examples</u> of the sorts of advice you could be asked to write in your exam:

> • <u>Leaflets</u> e.g. how to find a good summer job
> • <u>Magazine and newspaper articles</u> e.g. how to eat a healthy diet
> • <u>Speeches</u> e.g. to advise new pupils how to survive in your school
> • <u>Magazine features</u> e.g. a problem page for teenagers

Dear Jim, yes it is hard looking this smug
all the time. My advice would be...

Written Advice needs to be Reassuring

1) Written advice has got to get the <u>reader's attention</u>. A good <u>heading</u> would do the trick.

2) It's got to be <u>clear</u> what the advice is <u>about</u> (e.g. from the heading) so that people can decide whether or not they should read it. A leaflet on healthy eating is no good if it <u>looks</u> like it's a leaflet on bike maintenance...

3) Finally, if the reader is going to take your advice, they need to feel that you <u>understand</u> the issue thoroughly. You can convince them by using a <u>reassuring tone</u> throughout the text:

> Remember — you're not on your own.
> There are lots of people you can turn to who
> understand what it's like to be bullied.

Written advice suggests what Action to take

So... when you're writing your advice, you need to get the reader's <u>attention</u>, show you <u>understand</u> their feelings, and then, finally, you can actually give them your <u>advice</u>.

1) When you're writing to advise, you need to suggest to the reader what <u>courses of action</u> they could take.

2) You could give them a <u>range</u> of different <u>options</u> so they have some <u>choice</u>.

3) Then it's all up to the <u>reader</u> to take your advice... or not.

> You must tell someone if you're being bullied.

> This could be:
> • your parents
> • one of your teachers
> • your best friend
> • your doctor

My parents call it advising... I call it nagging...

State what you're going to advise on, reassure the reader and then give them an action plan. With these three little steps you too can fulfil your life's ambition and become an agony aunt.

Writing Style

Writing to advise is a bit like <u>archery</u> — you need to know what (well, who) you're aiming at. You're more likely to get your <u>advice</u> across if you write to your <u>audience</u> in the right way.

The writing style will depend on the Audience

You need to know <u>who</u> you're aiming your advice at. The <u>style</u> of language you use will depend on who your <u>audience</u> is. For example:

> Write an advice leaflet for victims of school bullying.

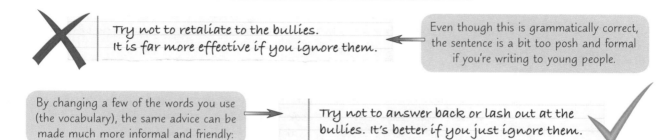

Try not to retaliate to the bullies. It is far more effective if you ignore them.

Even though this is grammatically correct, the sentence is a bit too posh and formal if you're writing to young people.

By changing a few of the words you use (the vocabulary), the same advice can be made much more informal and friendly:

Try not to answer back or lash out at the bullies. It's better if you just ignore them.

The more you adapt your <u>writing style</u> to your target audience, the more <u>relevant</u> your writing will seem to the reader, and the more they'll <u>pay attention</u> to your <u>advice</u>.

The writing style also depends on What the advice is About

If you're writing to advise on <u>serious</u> topics where you want to sound knowledgeable and <u>professional</u> rather than just reassuring, it's best to write in a <u>formal</u> style.

E.g. A lawyer may say: | I advise you, my client, to relinquish all rights to the property in question.

rather than: | I think you should give up the house.

Tell the reader their Options

When writing to advise, you need to <u>tell</u> the reader what <u>possible options</u> they've got (using words like '<u>could</u>'), as well as saying what you think they <u>should</u> do. There are many words you can use to do this. Here's an example:

shall should would must could can will may might

You could revise with friends, use a revision website, or do lots of practice questions, but whatever you do, you must put in at least an hour's revision a day.

Connect with the audience — they'll get their lighters out...

Texts that advise tend to assume the reader's already on the writer's side. People usually read them because they want to know about something and they trust the writer's opinion. Because of this, they usually sound more friendly and less 'in-your-face' than texts that argue or persuade.

Structure and Techniques

Here's some <u>handy stuff</u> to help you when you're writing to <u>advise</u>.

Use Headings and Bullet Points

Use <u>headings</u>, <u>sub-headings</u> and <u>bullet points</u> to <u>separate</u> different points of advice. Make sure you still have <u>well-developed</u> paragraphs though — don't split your writing into too many short sections.

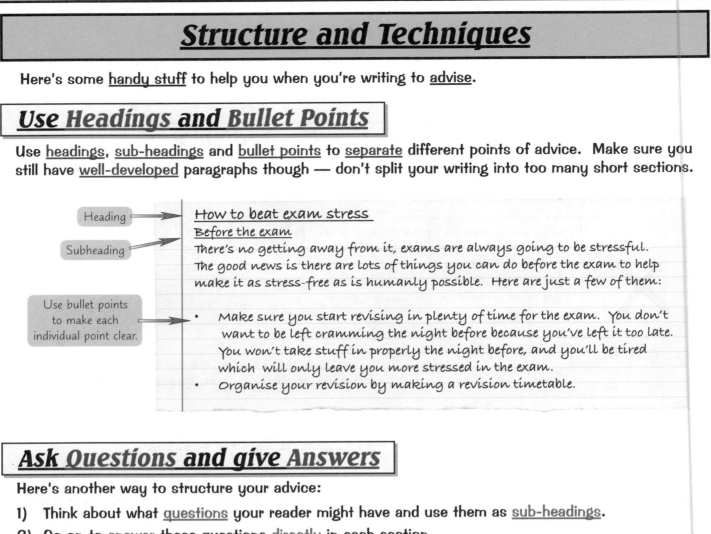

Heading →

Subheading →

How to beat exam stress

Before the exam

There's no getting away from it, exams are always going to be stressful. The good news is there are lots of things you can do before the exam to help make it as stress-free as is humanly possible. Here are just a few of them:

Use bullet points to make each individual point clear. →

- Make sure you start revising in plenty of time for the exam. You don't want to be left cramming the night before because you've left it too late. You won't take stuff in properly the night before, and you'll be tired which will only leave you more stressed in the exam.
- Organise your revision by making a revision timetable.

Ask Questions and give Answers

Here's another way to structure your advice:

1) Think about what <u>questions</u> your reader might have and use them as <u>sub-headings</u>.

2) Go on to <u>answer</u> these questions <u>directly</u> in each section.

   E.g.

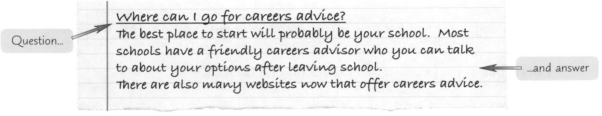

Question... →

Where can I go for careers advice?
The best place to start will probably be your school. Most schools have a friendly careers advisor who you can talk to about your options after leaving school.
There are also many websites now that offer careers advice.

← ...and answer

Say How, When, Where and Why

When you're writing to advise it's important to say <u>how</u>, <u>when</u>, <u>where</u> and <u>why</u> to take the advice you're giving. After all... if you're advising people to wear a <u>hard hat</u>, you want them to know to wear one at a building site, not all the time or just whenever they fancy it. That would be <u>silly</u>.

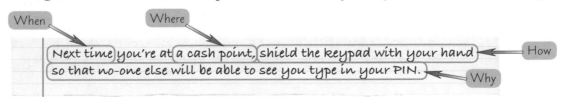

When   Where

Next time you're at a cash point, shield the keypad with your hand   ← How
so that no-one else will be able to see you type in your PIN.   Why

Where's the best place to hide from your teacher...

It's a bit like teaching a dog to do tricks.... sit, stay, heel, roll over, shake hands... Although I'm sure you won't be advising too many people to give you their paw for a doggy biscuit in your exam.

Writing Your Own

OK, now for <u>the scary bit</u> — what you'll actually have to do in your exam...

Before you start writing — Plan your answer

The writing to <u>advise</u> question might look something like this:

> Write an advice sheet for new Year 7 pupils, advising them on how to cope at a new school.

I'm sure you're raring to go, but before you dash off and write the <u>best advice</u> ever known to mankind, it's a good idea to <u>plan</u> your answer. For the Year 7 advice sheet, your plan might look like this:

1) It should include <u>all</u> the different points you want to cover in your answer. It can be useful to <u>separate</u> them using <u>bullet points</u>.

2) You can use your plan to work out the <u>order</u> of your points so your answer <u>flows</u> from one point to another.

3) <u>Check</u> your plan as you write your answer, to make sure you haven't <u>missed</u> anything.

Plan
Purpose = to advise
Form = advice sheet
Audience = Year 7
- School planner
- Lesson times
- Lunch and break time
- Uniform and equipment
- Homework
- Who to see if you have any problems

Write down Advising Techniques you know

While you're planning you might also want to jot down <u>advising techniques</u>. That way you'll be able to check back and make sure you've used them to make your answer effective and <u>well-structured</u>.

Plan — Advising techniques I know:
| you and your | questions and answers | reassuring tone |
| options | headings and bullet points | how, when, where, why |

Always start with an Introduction

1) You'll need a main <u>heading</u> covering what you're about to write about.

2) Then comes the <u>masterpiece</u> of wit and <u>reassurance</u> that tells the reader <u>what</u> you're about to advise them on. This is your <u>introduction</u>. Remember <u>who</u> you're advising so you can talk to them <u>directly</u>, and remember to be <u>reassuring</u>. Here's an example:

Heading →
Show understanding. →

Starting Secondary School
You're probably feeling a bit scared about starting your new school. There's no need to worry because help is at hand. Follow this advice and you'll be settled in before you know it.

Talk directly to the reader.
Reassuring and informal tone

Hmmm... planning looks like as much fun as writing...

It's really important to plan what you're going to write, that way, you're not going to miss out any bits you meant to cover. It might feel like you're wasting time by not starting your answer for 5 minutes, but you'll write a better answer in the end. So there.

Writing Your Own

Even more techniques to use when writing to advise... Don't say I never give you anything.

Organise your Advice properly

Now it's time to get your agony aunt hat on and give your advice. The key things to remember are:

1) Use sub-headings to separate the main issues you want to cover. Using questions as sub-headings and then answering them in the section below can be a really useful technique.

2) Bullet points are really great for separating each point you want to make in a particular section. Make sure you still explain yourself properly though — don't just give a list.

3) Don't forget who you're aiming your advice at so you use the right style.

4) And finally, don't forget to finish it off with a conclusion which sums up all your points.
    Here's a lovely example to get you in the mood:

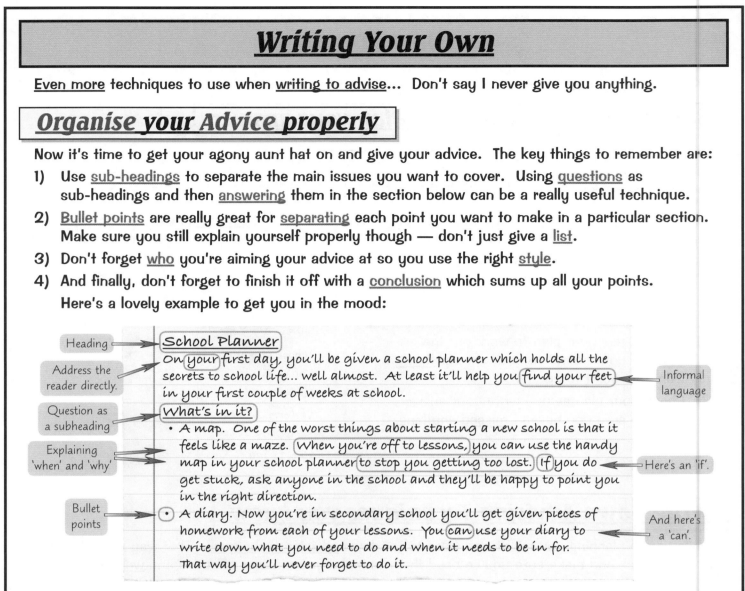

Heading → School Planner
Address the reader directly. → On your first day, you'll be given a school planner which holds all the secrets to school life... well almost. At least it'll help you find your feet in your first couple of weeks at school. ← Informal language

Question as a subheading → What's in it?
Explaining 'when' and 'why' → • A map. One of the worst things about starting a new school is that it feels like a maze. When you're off to lessons, you can use the handy map in your school planner to stop you getting too lost. If you do ← Here's an 'if'. get stuck, ask anyone in the school and they'll be happy to point you in the right direction.

Bullet points → • A diary. Now you're in secondary school you'll get given pieces of homework from each of your lessons. You can use your diary to ← And here's a 'can'. write down what you need to do and when it needs to be in for. That way you'll never forget to do it.

Gosh... who would have thought so many techniques could be used in such a small bit of writing.

Sum Up your advice at the End

1) Once you've written all your sound advice, all that's left to do is sum up your points.

2) It can often be useful to use bullet points, so the reader can quickly refer back to the main points of advice without having to read through the whole text again.

E.g.

Look at the lovely bullet points. → So if you're going to book a holiday, the most important things to remember are:
• Shop around. The first deal you see might look good but with a bit of browsing you can often find a better deal elsewhere.
• The earlier you book, the better. You can get the best holiday deals by booking either months in advance or going very last minute (when there's much less choice).
So if you know where you want to go, start looking early.

Now you can join Agony Aunts Anonymous...

Well, that's it. The fat lady is singing, and you've got to the end of 'writing to advise'. Keep calm in the exam, plan what you're going to include in your answer, make sure you know who you're writing to, and off you go. Now... I've got this problem... I wonder if you could advise me...

Summary of the Exam

There's just <u>one exam</u> for GCSE <u>English</u> and <u>English Language</u>. It's called <u>Unit 1</u>: Understanding and Producing Non-Fiction Texts. (You take <u>two other</u> units but you do these as <u>controlled assessments</u>.)

The Exam Paper is Split Up like this

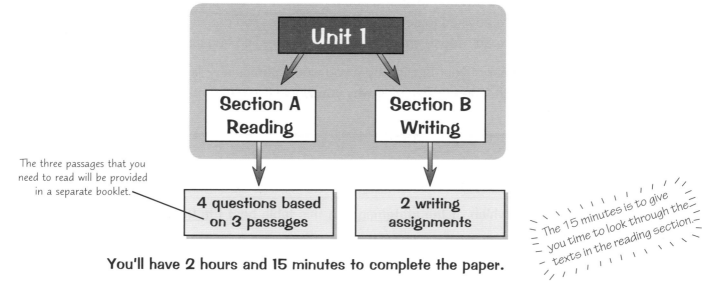

The three passages that you need to read will be provided in a separate booklet.

Unit 1
→ **Section A Reading** → **4 questions based on 3 passages**
→ **Section B Writing** → **2 writing assignments**

You'll have 2 hours and 15 minutes to complete the paper.

The 15 minutes is to give you time to look through the texts in the reading section.

Read all the Instructions on the paper Before You Start

1) Make sure that you have the <u>higher tier paper</u>, the one that has a <u>big capital H</u> on the <u>front cover</u>.
2) Before you start, read through <u>all the instructions</u> and advice on the front of the paper.
3) There will be an <u>invigilator</u> (probably one of your teachers) in the exam, who you can <u>ask for help</u> if the instructions aren't clear or you've been given the wrong paper.
4) Fill in all your <u>details</u> (like your <u>name</u> and <u>candidate number</u>) on the <u>front cover</u> of the exam paper.
5) Remember to write all your answers <u>on the pages provided</u> as part of the exam paper.

You must Answer All the Questions on this paper

1) For <u>Section A</u> you have to answer all <u>four</u> questions.
2) This section carries <u>40 marks</u> and you're advised to spend <u>one hour</u> on it.
3) <u>Section B</u> requires you to answer <u>both</u> questions, <u>5 and 6</u>.
4) <u>Question 5</u> carries <u>16 marks</u> and should take no more than <u>25 minutes</u>.
5) <u>Question 6</u> carries <u>24 marks</u> and you should spend about <u>35 minutes</u> on it.

- Before you close your paper and sit back and sigh, remember to <u>check</u> back over what you've written.
- This can be a <u>pain</u> after a long exam but you'd be surprised how many <u>silly mistakes</u> you'll spot.
- Try to read through each answer a <u>couple</u> of times and make any <u>corrections</u> as <u>neatly</u> as possible.

Ready? — I was born ready...

Knowing what you're in for is half the battle I reckon. There's nothing worse than getting a surprise in an exam so make sure you understand what you're going to have to do before you go in.

Exam Questions — Q5 and Mark Scheme

Section B of your exam paper will look like this:

> **Section B: Writing**
>
> *Don't just answer one of the questions!*
>
> Answer **both** questions in this section.
>
> You are advised to spend about one hour on this section.
>
> *Don't rush. Spend a few minutes planning your answers.*
>
> You are advised to spend about 25 minutes on question 5.
>
> You are advised to spend about 35 minutes on question 6.
>
> 5   There is a member of your family whom you would particularly like a friend to meet. Write a letter to the friend explaining why you would like him or her to come with you when you visit.

Here's a Mark Scheme telling you how to get each grade

The examiners will decide which of the statements in this table best fits your answer to Q5.

Grade	What you've written	How you've written	Spelling, punctuation and sentence structures
D/E	A few basic points with some use of writing techniques, e.g. repetition, rhetorical questions.	Fairly clearly written, with some use of paragraphs and awareness of purpose and audience. Standard English used.	Some simple and some complex sentences, common words spelt correctly, generally accurate use of full stops and capital letters.
C	More detailed points with appropriate tone, interesting vocabulary and some use of different writing techniques.	Written with clear structure, in paragraphs, and with a clear identification of purpose and audience. Clear development of ideas	Some fairly complex sentences, generally accurate spelling, good simple punctuation.
B	Good range of vocabulary and writing techniques to engage the reader.	Well structured, with form, content and style mostly matched to audience and purpose. Paragraphs used well, ideas well thought out and clearly presented and developed.	Some varied sentence choices, accurate spelling of most irregular and complex words, accurate and useful punctuation.
A.	Ambitious and imaginative vocabulary. Writing techniques used to engage the reader.	Fluently linked sentences and paragraphs consistently matching form, content and style to audience and purpose. Uses a variety of structural features.	Clear and controlled variation of sentence structures, accurate spelling, good range of accurate punctuation. Good range of vocabulary.
A*	Convincing, confident, compelling points combining a range of details, using writing techniques coherently. Complex, possibly abstract ideas.	Sophisticated structure that matches form, content and style to audience and purpose. Presents difficult ideas clearly.	Wide range of sentence structures successfully used for effect, sophisticated and accurate spelling and punctuation. Ambitious vocabulary.

Who the heck's Mark Scheme? — and why's he so fussy?

The last page tells you what the exam'll be like. This one tells you what the markers will be looking for in your answer. This stuff is so useful to know it almost feels like cheating (N.B. it's not).

Q5 Grade C & B Answers

Here are some <u>grade C and B</u> exam answers to the question on <u>page 42</u>.

This is a Grade C answer for Question 5

1) You are writing a <u>letter</u> to a <u>friend</u>, so you can use serious but friendly language.
2) You must <u>explain why</u> you want him or her to join you, so make sure you include lots of reasons.
3) Here's an extract from a <u>grade C</u> answer to show you what's needed.

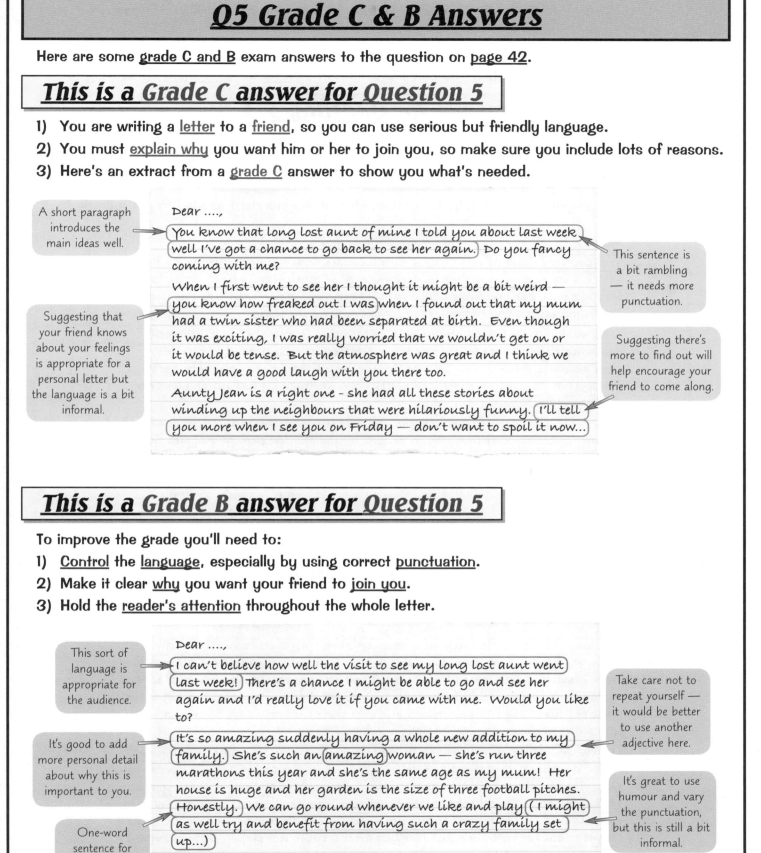

A short paragraph introduces the main ideas well.

> Dear ....,
>
> You know that long lost aunt of mine I told you about last week, well I've got a chance to go back to see her again. Do you fancy coming with me?
>
> When I first went to see her I thought it might be a bit weird — you know how freaked out I was when I found out that my mum had a twin sister who had been separated at birth. Even though it was exciting, I was really worried that we wouldn't get on or it would be tense. But the atmosphere was great and I think we would have a good laugh with you there too.
>
> Aunty Jean is a right one - she had all these stories about winding up the neighbours that were hilariously funny. I'll tell you more when I see you on Friday — don't want to spoil it now...

This sentence is a bit rambling — it needs more punctuation.

Suggesting that your friend knows about your feelings is appropriate for a personal letter but the language is a bit informal.

Suggesting there's more to find out will help encourage your friend to come along.

This is a Grade B answer for Question 5

To improve the grade you'll need to:
1) <u>Control</u> the <u>language</u>, especially by using correct <u>punctuation</u>.
2) Make it clear <u>why</u> you want your friend to <u>join you</u>.
3) Hold the <u>reader's attention</u> throughout the whole letter.

This sort of language is appropriate for the audience.

> Dear ....,
>
> I can't believe how well the visit to see my long lost aunt went last week! There's a chance I might be able to go and see her again and I'd really love it if you came with me. Would you like to?
>
> It's so amazing suddenly having a whole new addition to my family. She's such an amazing woman — she's run three marathons this year and she's the same age as my mum! Her house is huge and her garden is the size of three football pitches. Honestly. We can go round whenever we like and play (I might as well try and benefit from having such a crazy family set up...)
>
> Do you think that Ed might be interested in coming along too? I know his girlfriend's visiting him at the moment, but he seemed keen when I saw him last week, and I know he'd really appreciate Aunty Jean's unique brand of humour...

It's good to add more personal detail about why this is important to you.

One-word sentence for dramatic effect.

Take care not to repeat yourself — it would be better to use another adjective here.

It's great to use humour and vary the punctuation, but this is still a bit informal.

Saying that another friend thinks that it's a good idea might help convince your friend.

Q5 Grade A & A* Answers

Whether or not you're aiming for an A or an A*, it's definitely worth <u>having a glance</u> over the example answers on this page, then you can see what sort of <u>level</u> the <u>examiners</u> are looking for.

This is a Grade A answer for Question 5

1) At grade A your writing should be more <u>developed</u> and should <u>flow</u> beautifully.

2) Choose interesting <u>vocabulary</u> and be accurate with <u>punctuation</u> and <u>spelling</u>. Try to use a good variety of <u>sentence structures</u> too.

3) Look at this example extract, it will give you an idea of the standard needed to get a <u>grade A</u>:

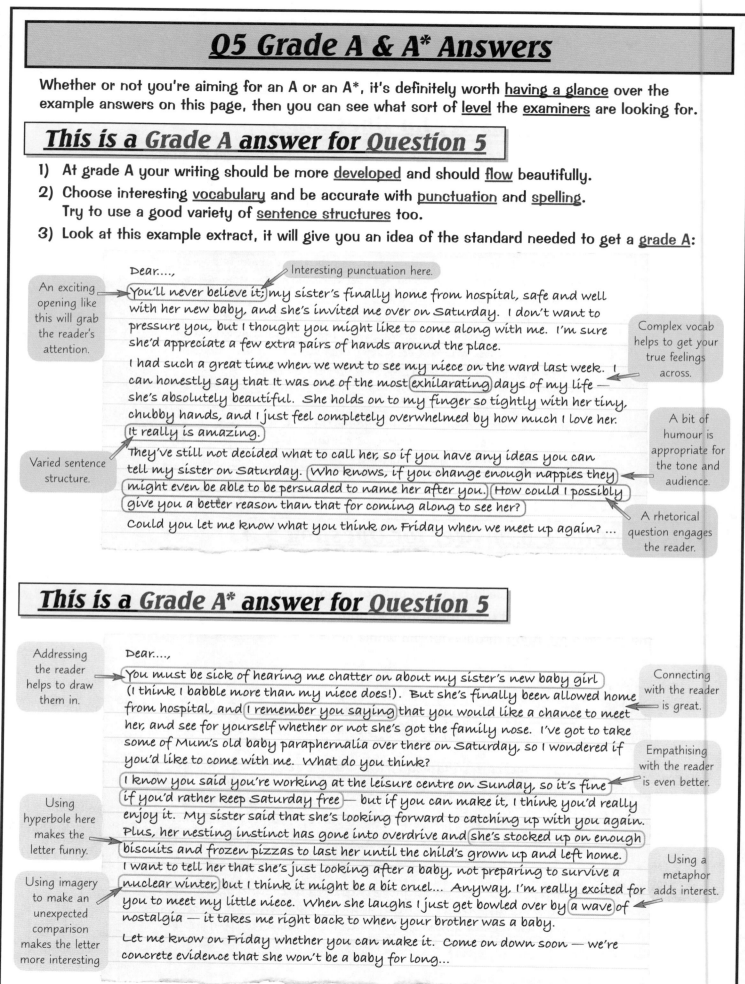

> Interesting punctuation here.

> An exciting opening like this will grab the reader's attention.

Dear....,

You'll never believe it; my sister's finally home from hospital, safe and well with her new baby, and she's invited me over on Saturday. I don't want to pressure you, but I thought you might like to come along with me. I'm sure she'd appreciate a few extra pairs of hands around the place.

I had such a great time when we went to see my niece on the ward last week. I can honestly say that it was one of the most exhilarating days of my life — she's absolutely beautiful. She holds on to my finger so tightly with her tiny, chubby hands, and I just feel completely overwhelmed by how much I love her. It really is amazing.

They've still not decided what to call her, so if you have any ideas you can tell my sister on Saturday. Who knows, if you change enough nappies they might even be able to be persuaded to name her after you. How could I possibly give you a better reason than that for coming along to see her?

Could you let me know what you think on Friday when we meet up again? ...

> Complex vocab helps to get your true feelings across.

> A bit of humour is appropriate for the tone and audience.

> Varied sentence structure.

> A rhetorical question engages the reader.

This is a Grade A* answer for Question 5

> Addressing the reader helps to draw them in.

Dear....,

You must be sick of hearing me chatter on about my sister's new baby girl (I think I babble more than my niece does!). But she's finally been allowed home from hospital, and I remember you saying that you would like a chance to meet her, and see for yourself whether or not she's got the family nose. I've got to take some of Mum's old baby paraphernalia over there on Saturday, so I wondered if you'd like to come with me. What do you think?

I know you said you're working at the leisure centre on Sunday, so it's fine if you'd rather keep Saturday free — but if you can make it, I think you'd really enjoy it. My sister said that she's looking forward to catching up with you again. Plus, her nesting instinct has gone into overdrive and she's stocked up on enough biscuits and frozen pizzas to last her until the child's grown up and left home. I want to tell her that she's just looking after a baby, not preparing to survive a nuclear winter, but I think it might be a bit cruel... Anyway, I'm really excited for you to meet my little niece. When she laughs I just get bowled over by a wave of nostalgia — it takes me right back to when your brother was a baby.

Let me know on Friday whether you can make it. Come on down soon — we're concrete evidence that she won't be a baby for long...

> Connecting with the reader is great.

> Empathising with the reader is even better.

> Using a metaphor adds interest.

> Using hyperbole here makes the letter funny.

> Using imagery to make an unexpected comparison makes the letter more interesting

Exam Questions — Q6 and Mark Scheme

After you've wowed the examiners on <u>Question 5</u>, you're just <u>one question</u> short of finishing your exam. All the way from Section B, weighing in at a whopping 24 marks, <u>Question... 6</u>.

You should spend about 35 Minutes on Question 6

1) Remember that you have to answer <u>both</u> questions in <u>section B</u>.
2) There are <u>24 marks</u> up for grabs for <u>Question 6</u>, so it's worth <u>spending a bit longer</u> on.
3) You'll be asked to write something to <u>argue</u>, <u>persuade</u> or <u>advise</u>.

6	'The media should not bother us with the private lives of celebrities, their families and their partners.' Write an article for a newspaper or magazine which argues for or against this idea.

Here's a Mark Scheme telling you how to get each grade

This <u>mark scheme</u> shows what the <u>examiners</u> look for when they're deciding what grade to give your answer. Just like for Q5, they'll decide which of the <u>statements</u> in this table <u>best fits your work</u>.

Grade	What you've written	How you've written	Spelling, punctuation and sentence structures
D/E	A few basic points with some use of writing techniques, e.g. repetition, rhetorical questions.	Fairly clearly written, with some use of paragraphs and awareness of purpose and audience. Standard English used.	Some fairly complex sentences, common words spelt correctly, some accurate use of full stops and capital letters.
C	More detailed points with appropriate tone, interesting vocabulary and some use of different writing techniques.	Written with clear structure, in paragraphs, and with a clear identification of purpose and audience. Clear development of ideas	Some fairly complex sentences, generally accurate spelling, good simple punctuation.
B	Good range of vocabulary and writing techniques to engage the reader. Viewpoint clearly sustained throughout the text.	Well structured, with form, content and style mostly matched to audience and purpose. Paragraphs used well, ideas well thought out and presented	Varied sentence choices, accurate spelling of most words, accurate and useful punctuation.
A	Ambitious and imaginative vocabulary. Writing techniques used to engage the reader with a clear awareness of opposing viewpoints.	Fluently linked sentences and paragraphs consistently matching form, content and style to audience and purpose. Answers show logic, persuasive thoughts and creativity.	Clear and controlled variation of sentence structures, accurate spelling, good range of accurate punctuation.
A*	Convincing, confident, compelling points combining a range of details, using writing techniques successfully. Complex, possibly abstract ideas presented effectively.	Sophisticated structure that matches form, content and style to audience and purpose (to argue, persuade or advise). Answers show logic, persuasive thoughts and creativity.	Wide range of sentence structures successfully used, sophisticated and accurate spelling and punctuation. Opposing viewpoints used for effect.

Q6 Grade C & B Answers

Here's a Grade C answer for Question 6

1) Aim to make your readers think.
2) Deal with counter arguments (ideas that disagree with yours) and make them look stupid.
3) Try to leave your readers with a comment that will keep them thinking about what you've written.

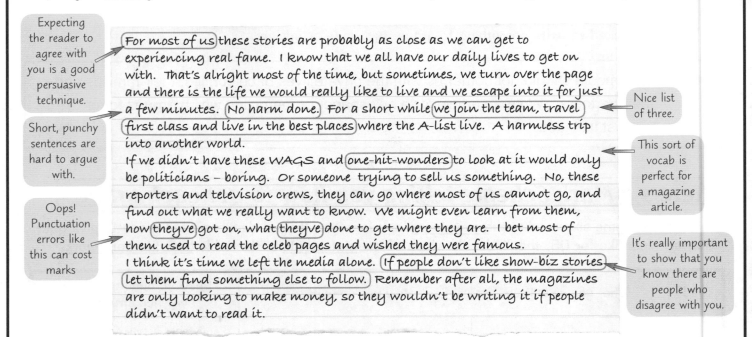

Expecting the reader to agree with you is a good persuasive technique.

Short, punchy sentences are hard to argue with.

Oops! Punctuation errors like this can cost marks

For most of us these stories are probably as close as we can get to experiencing real fame. I know that we all have our daily lives to get on with. That's alright most of the time, but sometimes, we turn over the page and there is the life we would really like to live and we escape into it for just a few minutes. No harm done. For a short while we join the team, travel first class and live in the best places where the A-list live. A harmless trip into another world.

If we didn't have these WAGS and one-hit-wonders to look at it would only be politicians – boring. Or someone trying to sell us something. No, these reporters and television crews, they can go where most of us cannot go, and find out what we really want to know. We might even learn from them, how they've got on, what they've done to get where they are. I bet most of them used to read the celeb pages and wished they were famous.

I think it's time we left the media alone. If people don't like show-biz stories let them find something else to follow. Remember after all, the magazines are only looking to make money, so they wouldn't be writing it if people didn't want to read it.

Nice list of three.

This sort of vocab is perfect for a magazine article.

It's really important to show that you know there are people who disagree with you.

Here's a Grade B answer for Question 6

1) You have to form an opinion and stick to it. Don't go changing your mind half way through.
2) You have to set out your arguments clearly.
3) Remember, you don't know your reader's opinion, so you should persuade them that yours is right.

Words like WAG are perfect for this sort of article.

Emotive language is brilliant for persuading your audience.

They just smile back at the camera, only too pleased that someone is taking notice of them. What have they done? What's so special about them? Why should we be the slightest bit interested in their lives? What about all those women who aren't WAGS, who can't roar off to the hairdressers in some flash car? They hold down demanding jobs and bring up families and nobody even cares. Real women getting on with real life, would make much better role models for young girls. Don't be fooled, any old twenty-something woman would look just as glamorous after hours of make-up and air-brushing. Perhaps if we ignored the celebs and their pathetic problems they'd go away to whatever hole they crawled out from.

Another thing, they're here today and gone tomorrow but they still want to get taken seriously. Why? What have they done except get their pictures taken? Why doesn't someone take mine? — I'm just as insignificant. No, if they want people to stare at them they should go and live in a zoo. Some people argue that magazines wouldn't cover celebrity stories if people didn't want to read them. That is not the point. Encouraging people to slobber over celebrity lifestyles is pathetic, unethical and wrong.

Rhetorical questions are great but be careful not to use too many.

This sort of repetition helps the article to flow.

Acknowledge counter-arguments and then disagree with them.

Nice list of three.

Q6 Grade A & A* Answers

Here's a Grade A answer for Question 6

1) To get an <u>A grade</u> in writing to <u>argue</u>, it's a good idea to include some <u>counter-arguments</u>. You'll also need to write <u>fluently</u>, <u>effectively</u> and <u>link</u> your paragraphs together well.

2) Here's an extract from a <u>grade A</u> answer to <u>question 6</u>.

Strong opening shows exactly where your argument's heading.

Rhetorical questions introduce points well.

Acknowledging other opinions makes you seem more convincing.

Powerful metaphor.

It's telling that the lives of these so-called 'celebrities' aren't exactly tales of hard graft or triumph over adversity. We never hear about how someone's selfless dedication to a charity over a period of years has brought them recognition. Instead we get self-important non-entities congratulating themselves for winning £1000 for charity on a gameshow (while neatly raising their own profile of course. "Oh the fame? It's just a by-product of my good works, darling. Gets in the way really...") Just what does one have to do to join the mystical heights of 'celebrity status'? If it involves nothing more than being the centre of attention then surely we should all have a turn. I accept that there is a certain demographic which demands this sort of nonsensical drivel, but there's no excuse for newspapers disappointing their readers hoping for serious news by presenting them with yet another grinning idiot. We should have kept this away from the respectable media, and halted the spread of this infection before people started caring what colour socks David Beckham's wearing. As it is, I'm afraid it's now far, far too late...

Using a sarcastic quote makes the people who disagree look stupid.

Well-timed use of humour can work really well.

Here's a Grade A* answer for Question 6

In an <u>A*</u> answer, examiners are looking for a real sense of <u>engagement</u>, almost <u>passion</u>, in what you write. Your argument needs to be <u>strong</u> and <u>convincing</u>. You need to sound as if you really <u>believe</u> in what you're writing about. Here's part of an A* response to the "<u>writing to argue</u>" question.

Metaphors make your answer more interesting.

Lists of three help the text flow smoothly

Of course you could argue that the lives of boy band members and WAGs have no place in the public consciousness. You could even argue that the media has an ethical duty not to give these people status that they don't deserve and inevitably can't handle. But that is no reason to become stuck up or snobbish about people whose only claim to fame is being famous. For a start, these dazzling reality show stars provide an important service for modest civilians whose lives would be the poorer without the occasional indulgent wallow in some C-list dirt. It might seem like a big claim, but I would argue that followers of celebrities find their lives enriched by their involvement in the lives of others. Having public figures who people can collectively discuss, adore and despise, serves to unite vast swathes of the population. What's more, on a serious note, public and media responses to the actions of famous people can teach important moral lessons and highlight the implications of certain behaviour: generosity or infidelity, for example. "Sounds like gossip" I hear you say. Well, you may be right, but then gossip can be the beginning of an interest in other people and the trials and tribulations they face in their lives. Cultivated and nurtured, a healthy interest in other people's dirty laundry can have a positive effect on your own life, because you can reassure yourself that at least you haven't got it as bad as them. And that is not something to be sniffed at.

Recognising opposing ideas shows that your viewpoint is carefully considered.

Nice sophisticated vocabulary.

Address the reader directly.

The ironic tone of this article makes it convincing and amusing.

Writing About Moving Images

Writing about what? It just means 'Here's a great chance to <u>show off</u> all those <u>sophisticated</u> writing techniques that you've picked up in the rest of the book by writing about <u>movies</u> and <u>TV shows</u>'.

You might have to Write a Film Review

1) You need to provide <u>factual information</u> about the film — e.g. what it's about and how long it is.

2) You also need to think about <u>who you're writing for</u> and whether you think <u>they'd</u> enjoy the film.

3) <u>Persuasive language</u> is useful if you're trying to <u>convince</u> people to go and see it.

Using film jargon like 'FX' makes you sound authoritative.

Lists of three can be used to build up excitement.

This triple-Oscared sci-fi romp has literally groundbreaking FX. Galaxies explode, new worlds are discovered and alien forces do battle, all to a mind-blowing score. Dare you watch in 3D?

You can engage the reader by addressing them directly using a rhetorical question.

You could be writing a Script or a Voice-over

<u>Voice-overs</u> and <u>scripts</u> for dialogue pop up all over — in <u>soaps</u>, <u>cartoons</u>, <u>adverts</u> and <u>documentaries</u>. You need to <u>adapt</u> the <u>tone</u> to suit the <u>purpose</u> of your piece.

Blind fish swimming
Isolated for generations in a network of caves beneath the Rio Grande, the Mexican Tetra has developed several unique adaptations to life in a world without light. These individuals have no eyes and every member of the population is an albino...

Documentary scripts should give the voice-over person chance to take a breath.

Offer plenty of informative 'factual' detail.

You could write a Short Story for a Film to be Based On

You might find yourself having to write a <u>text</u> that will be <u>adapted</u> for the screen. This could be for a <u>film</u> or <u>TV drama</u>. These texts need to have <u>detailed descriptions</u> to give the <u>director</u> a good idea of how you imagine the <u>characters</u> and <u>settings</u>.

This gives loads of visual detail that the director could use when making the film.

Late one misty Bristol evening in autumn 1879, Dr Procktar — no stranger to the sights, sounds and smells around its bustling wharves and taverns — headed to the quayside. As always, he wore his trademark battered brown overcoat, the frayed bullet hole in the left lapel, now a vivid reminder of how fortunate he had been in Munich, just two months earlier...

Describe the lead character to give the director clues.

Sets up a possible flashback and suggests more settings.

Battle Royale — based on a true story...

If a picture says a thousand words and a film is shot at 24 frames a second and lasts 162 minutes — I make that two-hundred and thirty three million, two hundred and eighty thousand words. Woah.

Writing on a Particular Theme

You might choose to do a 'commissions' piece if you're taking English Language. If you're taking English, you might choose a 'prompts' question. Either way, you could have to write on a theme.

Some Themes are Open to Interpretation

1) You might be asked to write on a theme that the examiners have made deliberately ambiguous.

2) They could use words that have more than one meaning, or use really broad topics.

3) The question below is an example of the sort of thing you might get.

> Write a creative piece on the theme 'The Four Seasons'

4) There's probably a few things that spring to mind straight away — so scribble them down.

5) Once you've jotted down all you can think of, you can decide which idea you want to write about.

6) When you've made your mind up, you can start thinking about the purpose of your text, what form it'll take and who you're writing it for.

How I grew up
Pizza
School year
12-month story
Garden
4 SEASONS
Love affair
Changing Landscape
Classical music
Beauty Site
Vivaldi

Other Themes can be a lot more Specific

1) You might choose a task where you have to do a particular type of creative writing.

2) On these types of question, you don't really have a chance to interpret the theme and your purpose, form or audience may have already been decided for you.

3) Have a look at the questions below for an idea of the kinds of things you might get:

Write a story beginning with the line: "That's the last time I ever ...', said X'

Purpose: describe/inform
Form: anecdotal narrative
Audience: general readers

Write a hobby-based article for your school or club website.

Purpose: inform (& persuade?)
Form: Online article, so factual prose
Audience: School community / visitors

Create text for a leaflet with one main slogan, such as EAT HEALTHILY, STAY CLEAN or RIDE SAFELY.

Purpose: inform, explain, persuade, remind
Form: snappy sentences
Audience: primary-age children?

It's easier than writing about Ham and Pineapple...

Being asked to 'write on a theme' is a bit daunting. But if you plan your answer before you start writing and always bear in mind your purpose, form and audience, you can't go too far wrong.

Changing the Genre of a Text

Believe it or not, changing a text's genre can actually be quite fun. I expect that you have chosen not to believe it, but you'll need to be able to do it anyway — so you may as well read this page...

You might change a Play or Poem into a Short Story...

1) Turning a piece into a short story gives you the chance to expand on things that are only hinted at in the original text.

2) You can combine information from the dialogue, characterisation and stage directions in plays, and from the feelings and themes expressed in a poem.

3) Remember to think about your narrative viewpoint — e.g. you could change the narrative so it's written from the point of view of one of the characters.

4) You could also change the tense — e.g. re-write something in the past tense.

5) Here's an example of how you could change a scene from Macbeth into a short story:

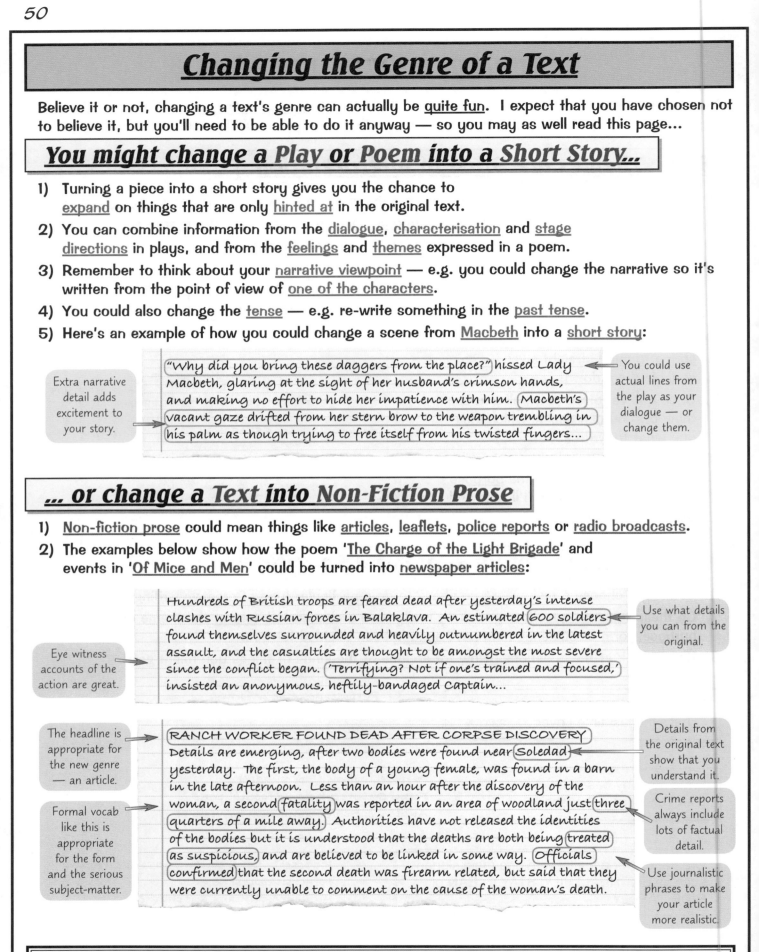

Extra narrative detail adds excitement to your story.

"Why did you bring these daggers from the place?" hissed Lady Macbeth, glaring at the sight of her husband's crimson hands, and making no effort to hide her impatience with him. Macbeth's vacant gaze drifted from her stern brow to the weapon trembling in his palm as though trying to free itself from his twisted fingers...

You could use actual lines from the play as your dialogue — or change them.

... or change a Text into Non-Fiction Prose

1) Non-fiction prose could mean things like articles, leaflets, police reports or radio broadcasts.

2) The examples below show how the poem 'The Charge of the Light Brigade' and events in 'Of Mice and Men' could be turned into newspaper articles:

Eye witness accounts of the action are great.

Hundreds of British troops are feared dead after yesterday's intense clashes with Russian forces in Balaklava. An estimated 600 soldiers found themselves surrounded and heavily outnumbered in the latest assault, and the casualties are thought to be amongst the most severe since the conflict began. 'Terrifying? Not if one's trained and focused,' insisted an anonymous, heftily-bandaged Captain...

Use what details you can from the original.

The headline is appropriate for the new genre — an article.

Formal vocab like this is appropriate for the form and the serious subject-matter.

RANCH WORKER FOUND DEAD AFTER CORPSE DISCOVERY
Details are emerging, after two bodies were found near Soledad yesterday. The first, the body of a young female, was found in a barn in the late afternoon. Less than an hour after the discovery of the woman, a second fatality was reported in an area of woodland just three quarters of a mile away. Authorities have not released the identities of the bodies but it is understood that the deaths are both being treated as suspicious, and are believed to be linked in some way. Officials confirmed that the second death was firearm related, but said that they were currently unable to comment on the cause of the woman's death.

Details from the original text show that you understand it.

Crime reports always include lots of factual detail.

Use journalistic phrases to make your article more realistic.

Adapt the text to a script for 'George and Lennie On Ice'...

This may be hard to come to terms with — but, all the fun stuff, like making your text look like the front page of a newspaper, doesn't count for any marks in the assessment so don't waste time on it.

Writing from Your Point of View

Writing from your <u>own</u> point of view is really important if you're doing <u>English</u>. If you're doing <u>English Language</u>, the examiners are less focussed on it — but it's still a <u>really useful skill</u> so stick around...

You might write about a Memory or a Personal Opinion

Writing from your <u>own viewpoint</u> can be trickier than it might seem. As always, you need to think about <u>who</u> you're writing for and the <u>purpose</u> of the piece you are writing. If you can write in any <u>form</u>, think about what's best for <u>getting your feelings across</u>.

1) If you're writing about your personal <u>opinions</u>, think carefully about the specific <u>details</u> or <u>events</u> that led you to have that particular viewpoint.

2) You should try to include lots of <u>personal anecdotes</u> — you can <u>make them up</u> if you like but it's easier if you've got some real ones that you could <u>relate</u> to.

3) Try not to be <u>shy</u> about expressing <u>emotion</u>, <u>warmth</u> or <u>pain</u>. If you feel strongly about something, let it come across in your writing — it'll probably make your piece a lot more <u>powerful</u>.

4) If you're <u>describing</u> something, like a <u>place</u> or a <u>person</u>, think about your different <u>senses</u>. It's easy to describe how something <u>looks</u>, but think about <u>sounds</u>, <u>smells</u>, <u>textures</u> and <u>tastes</u> as well.

Have a look at these Example Tasks

Some forms are really well-suited for getting personal feelings across — e.g. <u>blogs</u>, <u>diary entries</u>, <u>speeches</u>. You could also write a <u>short story</u> or <u>'real-life' magazine article</u> — see below:

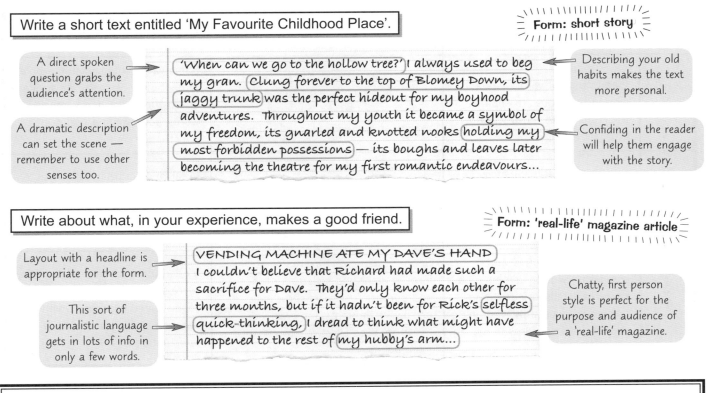

Write a short text entitled 'My Favourite Childhood Place'.

Form: short story

A direct spoken question grabs the audience's attention.

A dramatic description can set the scene — remember to use other senses too.

'When can we go to the hollow tree?' I always used to beg my gran. Clung forever to the top of Blomey Down, its jaggy trunk was the perfect hideout for my boyhood adventures. Throughout my youth it became a symbol of my freedom, its gnarled and knotted nooks holding my most forbidden possessions — its boughs and leaves later becoming the theatre for my first romantic endeavours...

Describing your old habits makes the text more personal.

Confiding in the reader will help them engage with the story.

Write about what, in your experience, makes a good friend.

Form: 'real-life' magazine article

Layout with a headline is appropriate for the form.

This sort of journalistic language gets in lots of info in only a few words.

VENDING MACHINE ATE MY DAVE'S HAND
I couldn't believe that Richard had made such a sacrifice for Dave. They'd only know each other for three months, but if it hadn't been for Rick's selfless quick-thinking, I dread to think what might have happened to the rest of my hubby's arm...

Chatty, first person style is perfect for the purpose and audience of a 'real-life' magazine.

This one time — at band camp...

When you tackle one of these questions, try and remember the four points in the purple box. At least this is one type of question where you've got no excuse for factual inaccuracies...

What You Have To Do — English Language

Your Unit 3b controlled assessment is like a cross between coursework and an exam.
It might not be much fun, but it does count for 15% of your overall GCSE, so it's worth doing well.

You get a Choice of Tasks for the Controlled Assessment

1) You have to write two pieces of creative writing, chosen from a bank of six topics.

2) You'll have up to 4 hours to write about 1200 words in total for the two pieces — they don't have to be of equal length (e.g. one could be 500 words and one could be 700 words).

3) You can use 'brief notes' during the final write-up, but not a whole draft.

4) You're allowed to look at external sources (e.g. dictionaries and the internet) while you're preparing, but not during the timed write-up.

5) Keep a careful record of any external references you use — you'll have to hand in your bibliography along with your final pieces of work.

6) Each piece is marked out of 10 for structure and content, with a further 10 marks overall for accuracy.

Here's a Mark Scheme telling you how to get each grade

This mark scheme shows what the markers look for when deciding which grade to give your piece of creative genius. They'll work out which of the statements in this table best fits your work.

Grade	What you've written	How you've written	Spelling, punctuation and sentence structures
C	Detailed points with appropriate tone, interesting vocabulary and some use of different writing techniques.	Written with clear structure, in paragraphs, and with some identification of purpose and audience.	Some fairly complex sentences, generally accurate spelling, good simple punctuation.
B	Good range of vocabulary and writing techniques to engage the reader. Sustained writing.	Well structured, with form, content and style mostly matched to audience and purpose. Paragraphs well organised and used to develop ideas.	Some varied and sometimes bold sentence choices, accurate spelling of most irregular and complex words, accurate and useful punctuation.
A	Ambitious and imaginative vocabulary. Writing techniques used creatively to engage the reader.	Fluently linked sentences and paragraphs consistently matching form, content and style to audience and purpose. Answers show logic, persuasive thoughts and creativity.	Clear and controlled variation of sentence structures, accurate spelling, good range of accurate punctuation.
A*	Convincing, confident and compelling writing combining a range of details, using writing techniques coherently. Complex, possibly abstract ideas presented effectively.	Sophisticated structure that matches form, content and style to audience and purpose. Answers show logic, persuasive thoughts and creativity. Structure used effectively to enhance main points.	Wide range of sentence structures successfully used for effect, sophisticated vocabulary with accurate spelling and correct punctuation.

On your marks... Get set... Go

Getting your head around what you'll be asked to do, and what the markers are looking for is half the battle. The other (arguably much harder) half simply involves giving the markers what they want.

Moving Images — Grade C & B Answers

Here are some examples of the <u>kinds of task</u> you might get, with <u>grade C and B</u> answers to them.

1) For this topic you'll have to write something <u>for</u> or <u>about</u> 'Moving Images'.
2) This means you'll have to think about the <u>pictures</u> that your language will <u>describe</u> or <u>create</u>.
3) Remember to get your answer clear in your head <u>before</u> you start — so think about your <u>purpose</u>, <u>form</u> and <u>audience</u>.

Here's a Sample Task and Grade C answer

Write an e-mail to a friend or relative abroad, persuading them to watch a particular new film or TV series you have enjoyed and explaining why you enjoyed it.

This opening is appropriate for the audience and form.

Chatty phrases like this are OK for an informal email, but you need more complex vocab to get top marks.

> Hi Bruce, how's life Down Under?
> Don't know what TV you get there but do watch out for a series we've just got called Procktar of the Docks. It's set in Bristol — so there are loads of shots of your old haunts. It's quite weird but really nice to see. You get a glimpse of our old school in the opening credits.
> Basically there's this mysterious Doctor who's a bit of a loner. He's been framed for his fiancée's murder and is trying to piece together the details of her death. Plenty going on, sets & costumes are quality and the guy playing the Doc is to die for! It was pretty confusing at first because there's tons of flashbacks but now I'm properly hooked — can't wait for next week's episode!

This should be in quotation marks.

Make sure you write full sentences.

Punctuation should be varied to show off your skills.

Here's a Sample Task and Grade B answer

Write the voice-over script for an advert to market a new consumer gadget that you have invented.

The use of stereotypes is a bit of a cliché, meaning you'll miss out on top marks.

Statistics, quotes from experts and scientific jargon can all be persuasive.

A clever slogan is the perfect ending.

> (Muscular, middle-aged man frowning at hairy shoulders in the mirror)
> Voice-over (macho voice): Like a dangerous animal, a man's shoulder hair needs to be restrained.
> (Man grinning as he shaves off the hair.)
> Voice-over: Harness the power of Gregson's Ultra-tech system and get behind the wheel of cutting-edge technology, originally developed by the army.
> (Man getting out of flashy pool and scooping up a pretty redhead in a bikini — cuts to close up of redhead)
> Redhead: 98% of women just like me say that using Ultra-tech made their boyfriends more handsome.
> (Shot of product spinning in space)
> Voice-over: Why not take a weight off your shoulders and take control of your life? Ultra-tech — landing on the shoulders of giants.

These words appeal specifically to the target audience.

Using a rhetorical question here engages the viewer.

Moving Images — Grade A & A* Answers

If you're after <u>top marks</u>, answers like the extracts on this page should be what you're aiming for. Remember to <u>plan</u> your answer before starting, thinking carefully about <u>form</u>, <u>audience</u> and <u>purpose</u>.

Here's a Sample Task and Grade A answer

Write the voice-over script for an advert to market a new consumer gadget that you have invented.

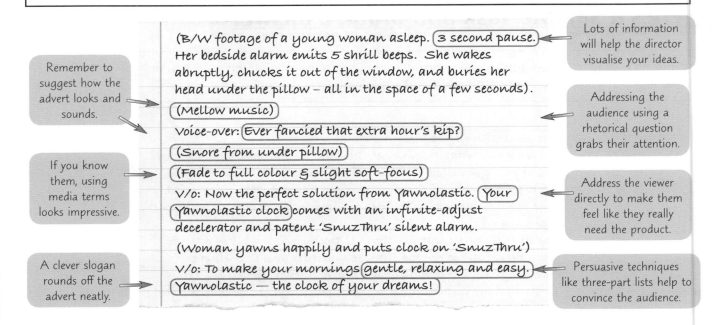

Here's a Sample Task and Grade A* answer

Write an e-mail to a friend or relative abroad, persuading them to watch a particular new film you have enjoyed and explaining why you enjoyed it.

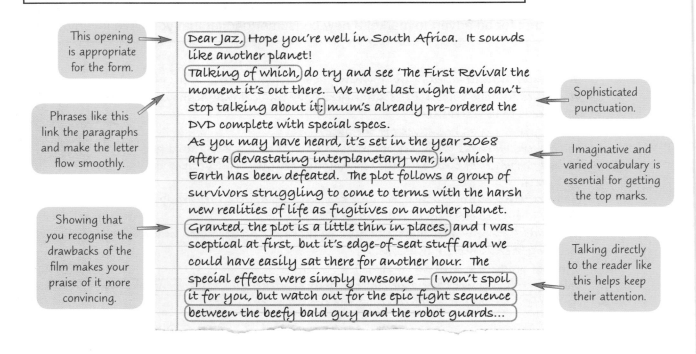

Commissions — Grade C & B Answers

Here are some examples of the <u>kinds of task</u> you might get, with <u>grade C and B</u> answers to them.

1) For this topic you'll be given a <u>commission</u> that you have to write something <u>for</u>.

2) It's like being a famous writer who's been asked to write something for a particular <u>reason</u>.

3) Remember to get your answer clear in your head <u>before</u> you start — so think about your <u>purpose</u>, <u>form</u> and <u>audience</u>.

Here's a Sample Task and Grade C answer

A local political organisation is holding a writing competition. You have to write a piece of prose with the title 'If I could change one thing...'

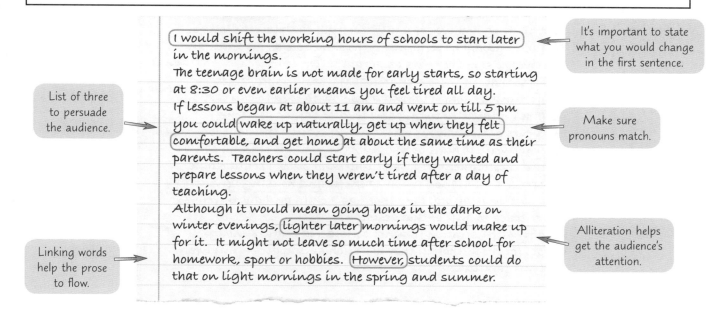

It's important to state what you would change in the first sentence.

List of three to persuade the audience.

Make sure pronouns match.

Linking words help the prose to flow.

Alliteration helps get the audience's attention.

I would shift the working hours of schools to start later in the mornings.
The teenage brain is not made for early starts, so starting at 8:30 or even earlier means you feel tired all day.
If lessons began at about 11 am and went on till 5 pm you could wake up naturally, get up when they felt comfortable, and get home at about the same time as their parents. Teachers could start early if they wanted and prepare lessons when they weren't tired after a day of teaching.
Although it would mean going home in the dark on winter evenings, lighter later mornings would make up for it. It might not leave so much time after school for homework, sport or hobbies. However, students could do that on light mornings in the spring and summer.

Here's a Sample Task and Grade B answer

An online charity is holding a writing competition. Write a piece of prose on the theme of 'Sacrifice'.

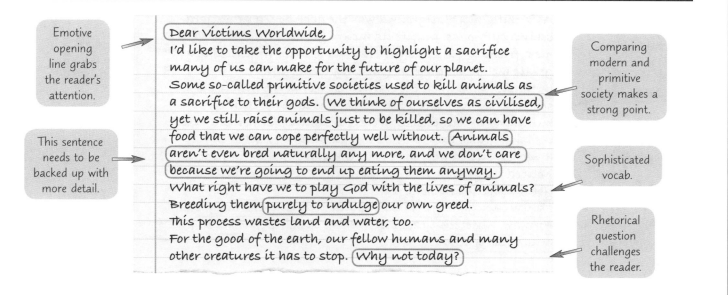

Emotive opening line grabs the reader's attention.

This sentence needs to be backed up with more detail.

Comparing modern and primitive society makes a strong point.

Sophisticated vocab.

Rhetorical question challenges the reader.

Dear Victims Worldwide,
I'd like to take the opportunity to highlight a sacrifice many of us can make for the future of our planet.
Some so-called primitive societies used to kill animals as a sacrifice to their gods. We think of ourselves as civilised, yet we still raise animals just to be killed, so we can have food that we can cope perfectly well without. Animals aren't even bred naturally any more, and we don't care because we're going to end up eating them anyway.
What right have we to play God with the lives of animals?
Breeding them purely to indulge our own greed.
This process wastes land and water, too.
For the good of the earth, our fellow humans and many other creatures it has to stop. Why not today?

SECTION EIGHT — THE CONTROLLED ASSESSMENT — ENGLISH LANGUAGE

Commissions — Grade A & A* Answers

Here are some lovely A and A* grade answers to give you an idea of the kind of thing you should be writing. Don't forget — think about <u>form</u>, <u>audience</u> and <u>purpose</u> before you start.

Here's a Sample Task and Grade A answer

A local political organisation is holding a writing competition. You have to write a piece of prose with the title 'If I could change one thing...'

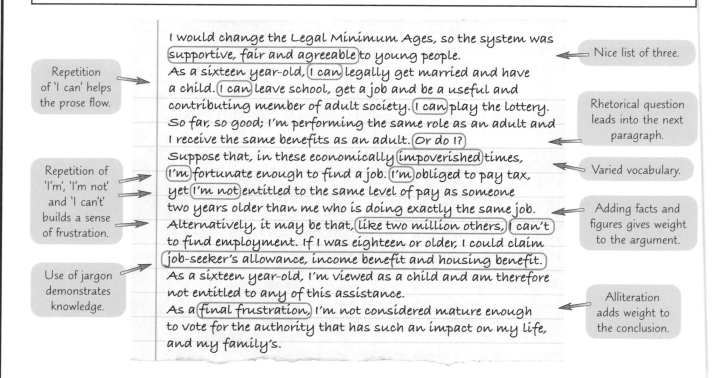

I would change the Legal Minimum Ages, so the system was supportive, fair and agreeable to young people.

As a sixteen year-old, I can legally get married and have a child. I can leave school, get a job and be a useful and contributing member of adult society. I can play the lottery. So far, so good; I'm performing the same role as an adult and I receive the same benefits as an adult. Or do I?

Suppose that, in these economically impoverished times, I'm fortunate enough to find a job. I'm obliged to pay tax, yet I'm not entitled to the same level of pay as someone two years older than me who is doing exactly the same job. Alternatively, it may be that, like two million others, I can't to find employment. If I was eighteen or older, I could claim job-seeker's allowance, income benefit and housing benefit. As a sixteen year-old, I'm viewed as a child and am therefore not entitled to any of this assistance.

As a final frustration, I'm not considered mature enough to vote for the authority that has such an impact on my life, and my family's.

- Repetition of 'I can' helps the prose flow.
- Repetition of 'I'm', 'I'm not' and 'I can't' builds a sense of frustration.
- Use of jargon demonstrates knowledge.
- Nice list of three.
- Rhetorical question leads into the next paragraph.
- Varied vocabulary.
- Adding facts and figures gives weight to the argument.
- Alliteration adds weight to the conclusion.

Here's a Sample Task and Grade A* answer

An online charity is holding a writing competition. Write a piece of prose on the theme of 'Sacrifice'.

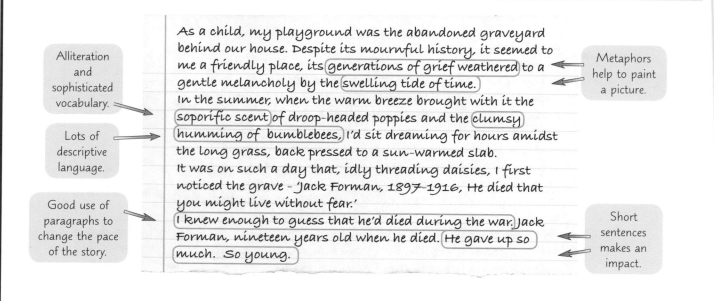

As a child, my playground was the abandoned graveyard behind our house. Despite its mournful history, it seemed to me a friendly place, its generations of grief weathered to a gentle melancholy by the swelling tide of time.

In the summer, when the warm breeze brought with it the soporific scent of droop-headed poppies and the clumsy humming of bumblebees, I'd sit dreaming for hours amidst the long grass, back pressed to a sun-warmed slab.

It was on such a day that, idly threading daisies, I first noticed the grave - 'Jack Forman, 1897-1916, He died that you might live without fear.'

I knew enough to guess that he'd died during the war. Jack Forman, nineteen years old when he died. He gave up so much. So young.

- Alliteration and sophisticated vocabulary.
- Lots of descriptive language.
- Good use of paragraphs to change the pace of the story.
- Metaphors help to paint a picture.
- Short sentences makes an impact.

Re-creations — Grade C & B Answers

Answering 'Re-creations' questions in the controlled assessment isn't too tricky. Have a look at the examples on these pages and you'll be well on your way to knowing how to pick up the marks.

1) For this topic you'll have to <u>change the genre</u> of a text that you're <u>familiar</u> with.

2) You might have to change a <u>poem</u> or part of a <u>novel</u> or <u>play</u> into <u>non-fiction</u> (e.g. an <u>article</u>).

3) Make sure you're comfortable with the <u>conventions</u> of the new genre that you'll be writing for. Think about how your <u>purpose</u>, <u>form</u> and <u>audience</u> might influence your choice of <u>language</u>.

Here's a Sample Task and Grade C answer

> Pick a key incident or character from any 20th-century text you have studied.
> Create a piece of non-fiction or journalism based on the issues raised in the original.

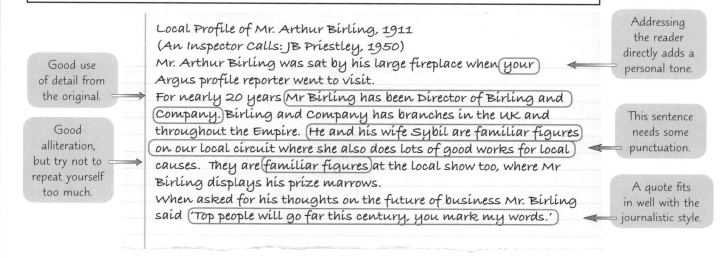

Local Profile of Mr. Arthur Birling, 1911
(An Inspector Calls: JB Priestley, 1950)
Mr. Arthur Birling was sat by his large fireplace when your Argus profile reporter went to visit.
For nearly 20 years Mr Birling has been Director of Birling and Company. Birling and Company has branches in the UK and throughout the Empire. He and his wife Sybil are familiar figures on our local circuit where she also does lots of good works for local causes. They are familiar figures at the local show too, where Mr Birling displays his prize marrows.
When asked for his thoughts on the future of business Mr. Birling said 'Top people will go far this century, you mark my words.'

Annotations:
- Good use of detail from the original.
- Good alliteration, but try not to repeat yourself too much.
- Addressing the reader directly adds a personal tone.
- This sentence needs some punctuation.
- A quote fits in well with the journalistic style.

Here's a Sample Task and Grade B answer

> Write a journalistic or non-fiction piece based on any well-known story of your choice.

COPS UNCOVER COBWEB CLUE
A police spokesperson today confirmed that the discovery of a cobweb has provided a vital lead in the hunt for missing schoolgirl, Miss Muffet. Concerns were first raised after the seven-year-old failed to return home after heading out for a picnic on Thursday afternoon. The cobweb, found by officers at Miss Muffet's favourite picnic spot, has been sent for forensic analysis and is believed to belong to a rare species of spider, which has a large body mass and threatening appearance.
Mr and Mrs Muffet have appealed for anyone with any information about their daughter's disappearance to come forward. "It's completely out of character — she's never done anything like this before," insisted Mrs Muffet, 35. Mr Muffet, said the family are hopeful that this latest development might prove helpful after revealing that Miss Muffet had arachnophobia.

Annotations:
- Alliteration in the headline is perfect for the genre.
- The factual tone adds humour, because this is usually a light-hearted story.
- Quotes are ideal for newspaper articles.
- Journalistic language shows that you understand the conventions of the new genre.
- Don't be afraid of making up extra characters or information.

Re-creations — Grade A & A* Answers

These A and A* answers are so <u>hot</u>, we had to get a special type of ink made just to stop them burning through the page. That's not actually true, but <u>they are really useful</u> — so take a look...

Here's a Sample Task and Grade A answer

Write a journalistic or non-fiction piece based on any well-known story of your choice.

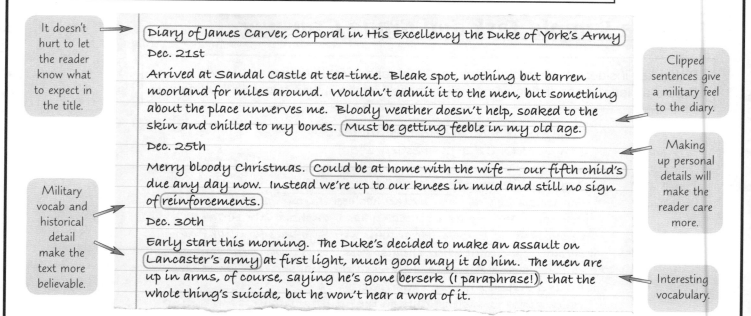

It doesn't hurt to let the reader know what to expect in the title.

Military vocab and historical detail make the text more believable.

Diary of James Carver, Corporal in His Excellency the Duke of York's Army

Dec. 21st

Arrived at Sandal Castle at tea-time. Bleak spot, nothing but barren moorland for miles around. Wouldn't admit it to the men, but something about the place unnerves me. Bloody weather doesn't help, soaked to the skin and chilled to my bones. Must be getting feeble in my old age.

Dec. 25th

Merry bloody Christmas. Could be at home with the wife — our fifth child's due any day now. Instead we're up to our knees in mud and still no sign of reinforcements.

Dec. 30th

Early start this morning. The Duke's decided to make an assault on Lancaster's army at first light, much good may it do him. The men are up in arms, of course, saying he's gone berserk (I paraphrase!), that the whole thing's suicide, but he won't hear a word of it.

Clipped sentences give a military feel to the diary.

Making up personal details will make the reader care more.

Interesting vocabulary.

Here's a Sample Task and Grade A* answer

Pick a key incident or character from any 20th-century text you have studied. Create a piece of non-fiction or journalism based on the issues raised in the original.

At first, this word seems a bit odd, but its significance is revealed at the end of the sentence.

Complex vocab.

A typical journalistic ending, combined with detail from the novel is perfect here.

Pigs Might Fly

History took a wobbly turn for Manor Farm (formerly Animal Farm) yesterday as its self-styled leader Napoleon became the first ever pig to face magistrates' bail on a drunken cycling charge. Responding to an anonymous tip-off after a spate of drink-fuelled disturbances, officers allegedly discovered Napoleon astride a lady's bicycle. He was found to have a breath alcohol level substantially exceeding the human safe driving limit. The bicycle, said to have insufficiently maintained lighting and brakes, together with a Crown Derby tureen and a quantity of home brewing apparatus, has been removed from the scene for forensic examination. Napoleon's spokesman, Squealer, was unavailable for comment.

A full report of the court case will follow in our next edition ...

'Newspaper-style' language is appropriate for the new genre.

It's fine to put in modern details to make the article more realistic or entertaining.

What You Have To Do — English

Your Unit 3b controlled assessment is like a cross between coursework and an exam.
It might not be much fun, but it does count for 20% of your overall GCSE, so it's worth doing well.

You get a Choice of Tasks for the Controlled Assessment

1) You have to write two pieces of creative writing, chosen from a bank of six topics.

2) You'll have up to 4 hours to write about 1600 words in total for the two pieces — they don't have to be of equal length (e.g. one could be 900 words and one could be 700 words).

3) You can use 'brief notes' during the final write-up, but not a whole draft.

4) You're allowed to look at external sources (e.g. dictionaries and the internet) while you're preparing, but not during the timed write-up.

5) Keep a careful record of any external references you use — you'll have to hand in your bibliography along with your final pieces of work.

6) Each piece is marked out of 15 for structure and content, with a further 15 marks overall for accuracy.

Here's a Mark Scheme telling you how to get each grade

This mark scheme shows what the markers look for when deciding which grade to give your piece of creative genius. They'll work out which of the statements in this table best fits your work.

Grade	What you've written	How you've written	Spelling, punctuation and sentence structures
C	Detailed points with appropriate tone, interesting vocabulary and some use of different writing techniques.	Written with clear structure, in paragraphs, and with some identification of purpose and audience.	Some fairly complex sentences, generally accurate spelling, good simple punctuation.
B	Good range of vocabulary and writing techniques to engage the reader. Sustained writing.	Well structured, with form, content and style mostly matched to audience and purpose. Paragraphs well organised and used to develop ideas.	Some varied and sometimes bold sentence choices, accurate spelling of most irregular and complex words, accurate and useful punctuation.
A	Ambitious and imaginative vocabulary. Writing techniques used creatively to engage the reader.	Fluently linked sentences and paragraphs consistently matching form, content and style to audience and purpose. Answers show logic, persuasive thoughts and creativity.	Clear and controlled variation of sentence structures, accurate spelling, good range of accurate punctuation.
A*	Convincing, confident and compelling writing combining a range of details, using writing techniques coherently. Complex, possibly abstract ideas presented effectively.	Sophisticated structure that matches form, content and style to audience and purpose. Answers show logic, persuasive thoughts and creativity. Structure used effectively to enhance main points.	Wide range of sentence structures successfully used for effect, sophisticated vocabulary with accurate spelling and correct punctuation.

On your marks... Get set... Go

Getting your head around what you'll be asked to do, and what the markers are looking for is half the battle. The other (arguably much harder) half simply involves giving the markers what they want.

Moving Images — Grade C & B Answers

You'll be able to choose <u>one</u> of <u>two</u> 'Moving Images' tasks if you fancy doing one. Have a look over these <u>grade C</u> and <u>B</u> example answers to get an idea of what you'll need to write.

1) For this topic you'll have to write something <u>for</u> or <u>about</u> 'moving images'.

2) This means you'll have to think about the <u>pictures</u> that your language will <u>describe</u> or <u>create</u>.

3) Remember to get your answer clear in your head <u>before</u> you start — so think about your <u>purpose</u>, <u>form</u> and <u>audience</u>.

Here's a Sample Task and Grade C answer

Write a short story with the title 'Flaming June', which could be adapted into a film script. Your writing should contain visual detail to help the film director.

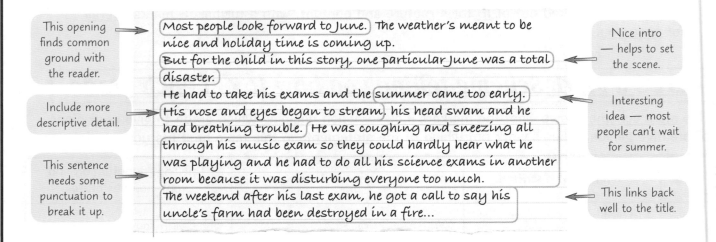

This opening finds common ground with the reader.

Most people look forward to June. The weather's meant to be nice and holiday time is coming up.

Nice intro — helps to set the scene.

But for the child in this story, one particular June was a total disaster.

Include more descriptive detail.

He had to take his exams and the summer came too early. His nose and eyes began to stream. his head swam and he had breathing trouble.

Interesting idea — most people can't wait for summer.

This sentence needs some punctuation to break it up.

He was coughing and sneezing all through his music exam so they could hardly hear what he was playing and he had to do all his science exams in another room because it was disturbing everyone too much.

The weekend after his last exam, he got a call to say his uncle's farm had been destroyed in a fire...

This links back well to the title.

Here's a Sample Task and Grade B answer

Write a descriptive piece based on a film you've seen.
You can focus your answer on a particular scene or character.

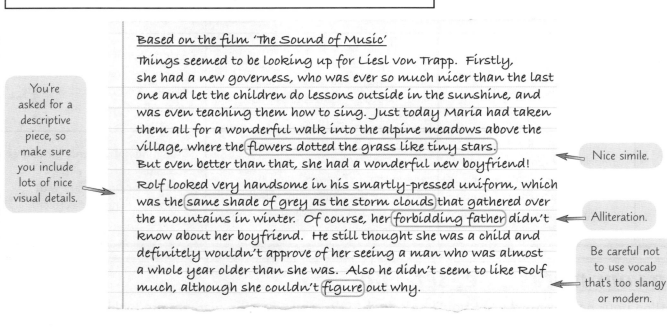

You're asked for a descriptive piece, so make sure you include lots of nice visual details.

Based on the film 'The Sound of Music'

Things seemed to be looking up for Liesl von Trapp. Firstly, she had a new governess, who was ever so much nicer than the last one and let the children do lessons outside in the sunshine, and was even teaching them how to sing. Just today Maria had taken them all for a wonderful walk into the alpine meadows above the village, where the flowers dotted the grass like tiny stars. But even better than that, she had a wonderful new boyfriend!

Nice simile.

Rolf looked very handsome in his smartly-pressed uniform, which was the same shade of grey as the storm clouds that gathered over the mountains in winter. Of course, her forbidding father didn't know about her boyfriend. He still thought she was a child and definitely wouldn't approve of her seeing a man who was almost a whole year older than she was. Also he didn't seem to like Rolf much, although she couldn't figure out why.

Alliteration.

Be careful not to use vocab that's too slangy or modern.

Moving Images — Grade A & A* Answers

Unbelievable — another two sample answers for you to drool over. These two are A and A* level, but the comments all still worth bearing in mind if you're aiming for a B or C Grade.

Here's a Sample Task and Grade A answer

> Write a short story with the title 'Flaming June', which could be adapted into a film script. Your writing should contain visual detail in order to help the film director.

Clever play-on-words — June the girl is 'flaming'.

List of three and personification of fire adds interest.

Now the character has been set up, the main plot is revealed.

Born on a searing midsummer afternoon, emerald-eyed, copperheaded June Hosier was pretty, bright and popular. She captained several school sports teams, and, ever eager to combine new experience with serving others, became the second-youngest D-of-E Golden Girl.

At 16, June took part in a college sports tour to Cuba, which gave her the opportunity to explore the tree-lined squares and sun-baked streets of Havana and the tropical wildness of the surrounding countryside. One night, when she was staying at a substandard hostel in the sprawling sugarcane plantations of Matanzas, a fire broke out. Other students panicked before the crackling, leaping, taunting blaze but June made sure everyone was safe.

This event awoke her ambition to join the Fire Service and become the first female Chief. Her crew colleagues said she was 'fit, focused and fun', but breaking the glass ceiling would be her very greatest challenge...

Using long sentences with ambitious structures shows that you're a confident writer.

Visual detail sets the scene.

Nice alliteration.

Here's a Sample Task and Grade A* answer

> Write a descriptive piece based on a film you've seen. You can focus your answer on a particular scene or character.

A punchy opening sentence that draws the reader in.

Short sentence and exclamation mark reflect Jack's excitement.

Using senses other than sight to create atmosphere is very effective.

Based on the film 'Titanic'

Jack Dawson was on top of the world! Last summer he'd been a struggling artist, trawling Paris for work, forced to bow and scrape to haughty men who barely saw him, on the off-chance they might commission him. Forced to flirt with middle-aged women who gazed at him lasciviously under half-lowered lashes, all for the privilege of painting their thickly-rouged faces and returning to them some measure of their lost youth. But now! A few too many brandies, a lucky hand at poker, and in the blink of an eye his life had changed beyond recognition... for when the RMS Titanic set sail for the New World, Jack Dawson would be on-board.

As far as Jack was concerned, the ship couldn't sail a moment too soon. Paris in summer had been muggy and oppressive, the labyrinth of ancient streets thronged with sightseers squabbling over shoddy souvenirs. And for a penniless artist, often without the funds for even a cool glass of beer, the charm had certainly worn off.

Repetition of 'forced' is really effective.

Sophisticated vocabulary.

Nice visual detail.

Good alliteration.

Prompts & Re-creations — Grade C & B Answers

The <u>Moving Images</u> questions give you a great chance to be <u>creative</u>, but if you don't fancy them, you could have a go at '<u>Prompts and Re-creations</u>' instead. Here are some <u>sample answers</u> for you.

1) For this topic you'll be given a <u>theme</u> or a <u>phrase</u> and you have to write something <u>based</u> on it.
2) Don't forget, you need to make sure your answer is <u>clear</u> in your head <u>before</u> you start writing — so come up with a <u>plan</u>, based on your <u>purpose</u>, <u>form</u> and <u>audience</u>.

Here's a Sample Task and Grade C answer

Write a short story which contains the phrase 'months stretched into years'.

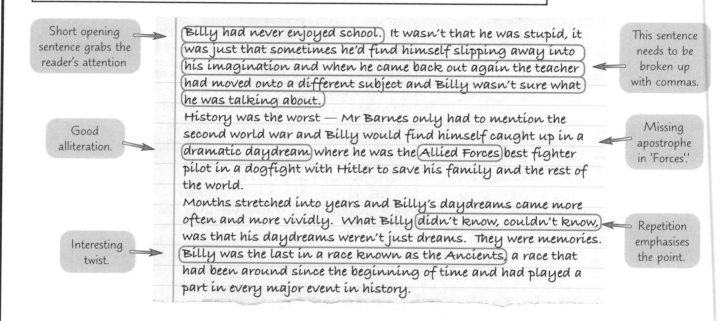

Short opening sentence grabs the reader's attention →

Billy had never enjoyed school. It wasn't that he was stupid, it was just that sometimes he'd find himself slipping away into his imagination and when he came back out again the teacher had moved onto a different subject and Billy wasn't sure what he was talking about.

← This sentence needs to be broken up with commas.

History was the worst — Mr Barnes only had to mention the second world war and Billy would find himself caught up in a dramatic daydream where he was the Allied Forces best fighter pilot in a dogfight with Hitler to save his family and the rest of the world.

Good alliteration. →

← Missing apostrophe in 'Forces'.

Months stretched into years and Billy's daydreams came more often and more vividly. What Billy didn't know, couldn't know, was that his daydreams weren't just dreams. They were memories. Billy was the last in a race known as the Ancients, a race that had been around since the beginning of time and had played a part in every major event in history.

Interesting twist. →

← Repetition emphasises the point.

Here's a Sample Task and Grade B answer

Use a scene or event from a Shakespeare play you have studied, and transform it into a piece of non-fiction or journalistic prose.

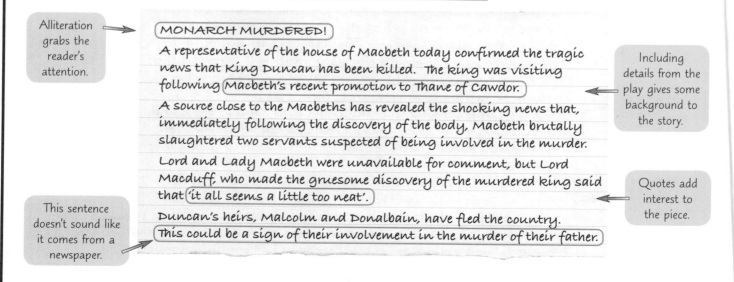

Alliteration grabs the reader's attention. →

MONARCH MURDERED!

A representative of the house of Macbeth today confirmed the tragic news that King Duncan has been killed. The king was visiting following Macbeth's recent promotion to Thane of Cawdor.

← Including details from the play gives some background to the story.

A source close to the Macbeths has revealed the shocking news that, immediately following the discovery of the body, Macbeth brutally slaughtered two servants suspected of being involved in the murder.

Lord and Lady Macbeth were unavailable for comment, but Lord Macduff, who made the gruesome discovery of the murdered king said that 'it all seems a little too neat'.

← Quotes add interest to the piece.

Duncan's heirs, Malcolm and Donalbain, have fled the country. This could be a sign of their involvement in the murder of their father.

This sentence doesn't sound like it comes from a newspaper. →

Prompts & Re-creations — Grade A & A* Answers

If you're aiming for an <u>A</u> or <u>A*</u>, then these are the answers that you really need to read carefully. But whatever you're aiming for, read the comments and try to incorporate them into your own work.

Here's a Sample Task and Grade A answer

Write a short story which contains the phrase 'months stretched into years'.

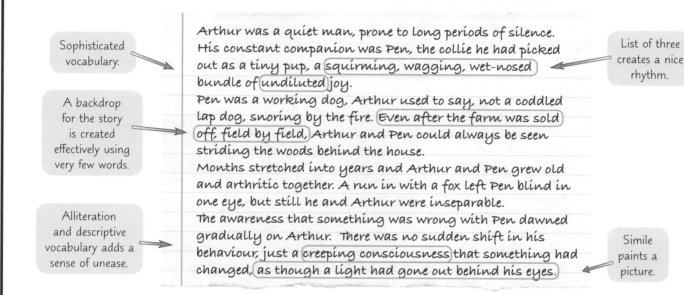

Sophisticated vocabulary.

A backdrop for the story is created effectively using very few words.

Alliteration and descriptive vocabulary adds a sense of unease.

Arthur was a quiet man, prone to long periods of silence. His constant companion was Pen, the collie he had picked out as a tiny pup, a squirming, wagging, wet-nosed bundle of undiluted joy.

Pen was a working dog, Arthur used to say, not a coddled lap dog, snoring by the fire. Even after the farm was sold off, field by field, Arthur and Pen could always be seen striding the woods behind the house.

Months stretched into years and Arthur and Pen grew old and arthritic together. A run in with a fox left Pen blind in one eye, but still he and Arthur were inseparable.

The awareness that something was wrong with Pen dawned gradually on Arthur. There was no sudden shift in his behaviour, just a creeping consciousness that something had changed, as though a light had gone out behind his eyes.

List of three creates a nice rhythm.

Simile paints a picture.

Here's a Sample Task and Grade A* answer

Use a scene or event from a Shakespeare play you have studied, and transform it into a piece of non-fiction or journalistic prose.

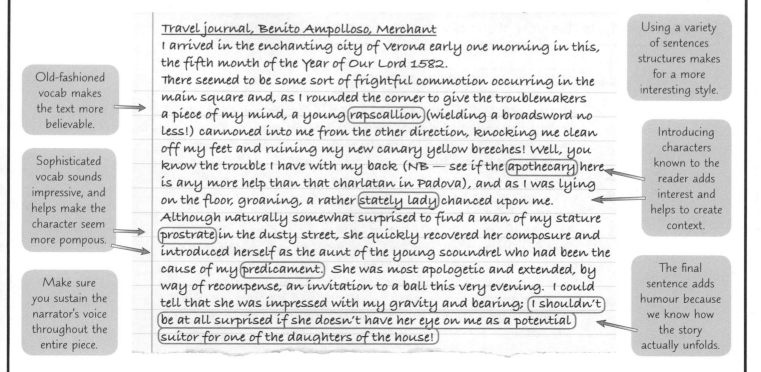

Old-fashioned vocab makes the text more believable.

Sophisticated vocab sounds impressive, and helps make the character seem more pompous.

Make sure you sustain the narrator's voice throughout the entire piece.

<u>Travel journal, Benito Ampolloso, Merchant</u>
I arrived in the enchanting city of Verona early one morning in this, the fifth month of the Year of Our Lord 1582.
There seemed to be some sort of frightful commotion occurring in the main square and, as I rounded the corner to give the troublemakers a piece of my mind, a young rapscallion (wielding a broadsword no less!) cannoned into me from the other direction, knocking me clean off my feet and ruining my new canary yellow breeches! Well, you know the trouble I have with my back (NB — see if the apothecary here is any more help than that charlatan in Padova), and as I was lying on the floor, groaning, a rather stately lady chanced upon me. Although naturally somewhat surprised to find a man of my stature prostrate in the dusty street, she quickly recovered her composure and introduced herself as the aunt of the young scoundrel who had been the cause of my predicament. She was most apologetic and extended, by way of recompense, an invitation to a ball this very evening. I could tell that she was impressed with my gravity and bearing; I shouldn't be at all surprised if she doesn't have her eye on me as a potential suitor for one of the daughters of the house!

Using a variety of sentences structures makes for a more interesting style.

Introducing characters known to the reader adds interest and helps to create context.

The final sentence adds humour because we know how the story actually unfolds.

Me, Myself, 1 — Grade C & B Answers

There are a couple of '<u>Me, Myself, I</u>' questions to choose from in the <u>GCSE English Unit 3</u>. I've rustled up these two pages of example tasks and answers <u>just for you</u> — so get stuck in.

1) If you choose one of these questions, you'll have to write something <u>from your own viewpoint</u>.

2) Being <u>honest</u> and using real <u>feelings</u> and <u>experiences</u> will make you sound <u>convincing</u>, but remember that you can <u>make them up</u> if you can't think of anything interesting to say.

Here's a Sample Task and Grade C answer

Write, in any form, about three objects you would choose to put in a time capsule, to be recovered in 50 years time. Write about why you chose these objects.

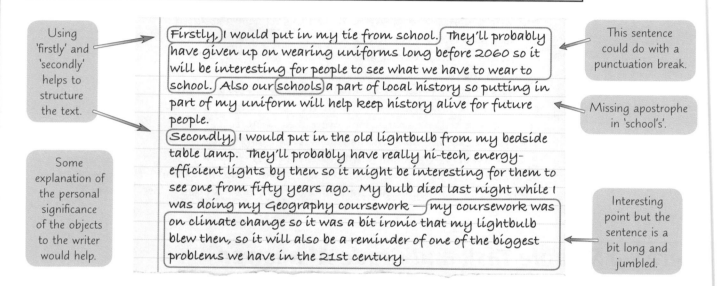

Using 'firstly' and 'secondly' helps to structure the text.

Some explanation of the personal significance of the objects to the writer would help.

Firstly, I would put in my tie from school. They'll probably have given up on wearing uniforms long before 2060 so it will be interesting for people to see what we have to wear to school. Also our schools a part of local history so putting in part of my uniform will help keep history alive for future people.

Secondly, I would put in the old lightbulb from my bedside table lamp. They'll probably have really hi-tech, energy-efficient lights by then so it might be interesting for them to see one from fifty years ago. My bulb died last night while I was doing my Geography coursework — my coursework was on climate change so it was a bit ironic that my lightbulb blew then, so it will also be a reminder of one of the biggest problems we have in the 21st century.

This sentence could do with a punctuation break.

Missing apostrophe in 'school's'.

Interesting point but the sentence is a bit long and jumbled.

Here's a Sample Task and Grade B answer

Using any form, tell the story of one of your most significant achievements so far.

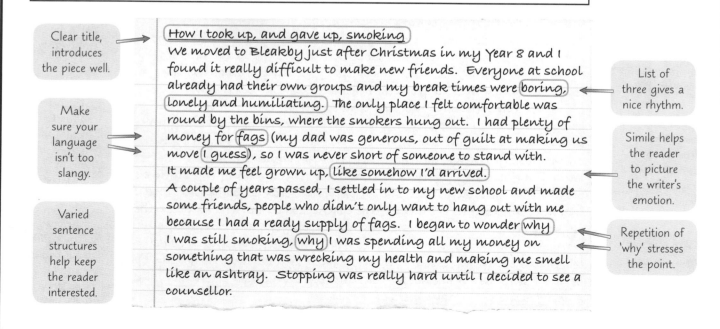

Clear title, introduces the piece well.

Make sure your language isn't too slangy.

Varied sentence structures help keep the reader interested.

How I took up, and gave up, smoking
We moved to Bleakby just after Christmas in my Year 8 and I found it really difficult to make new friends. Everyone at school already had their own groups and my break times were boring, lonely and humiliating. The only place I felt comfortable was round by the bins, where the smokers hung out. I had plenty of money for fags (my dad was generous, out of guilt at making us move I guess), so I was never short of someone to stand with. It made me feel grown up, like somehow I'd arrived.
A couple of years passed, I settled in to my new school and made some friends, people who didn't only want to hang out with me because I had a ready supply of fags. I began to wonder why I was still smoking, why I was spending all my money on something that was wrecking my health and making me smell like an ashtray. Stopping was really hard until I decided to see a counsellor.

List of three gives a nice rhythm.

Simile helps the reader to picture the writer's emotion.

Repetition of 'why' stresses the point.

Me, Myself, I — Grade A & A* Answers

You know the drill by now, have a look through these grade A and A* answers and pick out the kind of things you have to write if you're aiming for <u>top marks</u> in your <u>controlled assessment</u>.

Here's a Sample Task and Grade A answer

Using any form, tell the story of one of your most significant achievements so far.

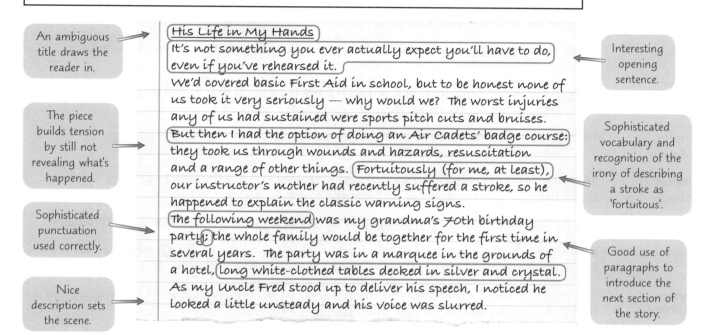

An ambiguous title draws the reader in.

The piece builds tension by still not revealing what's happened.

Sophisticated punctuation used correctly.

Nice description sets the scene.

His Life in My Hands

It's not something you ever actually expect you'll have to do, even if you've rehearsed it.

We'd covered basic First Aid in school, but to be honest none of us took it very seriously — why would we? The worst injuries any of us had sustained were sports pitch cuts and bruises. But then I had the option of doing an Air Cadets' badge course: they took us through wounds and hazards, resuscitation and a range of other things. Fortuitously (for me, at least), our instructor's mother had recently suffered a stroke, so he happened to explain the classic warning signs.

The following weekend was my grandma's 70th birthday party; the whole family would be together for the first time in several years. The party was in a marquee in the grounds of a hotel, long white-clothed tables decked in silver and crystal. As my Uncle Fred stood up to deliver his speech, I noticed he looked a little unsteady and his voice was slurred.

Interesting opening sentence.

Sophisticated vocabulary and recognition of the irony of describing a stroke as 'fortuitous'.

Good use of paragraphs to introduce the next section of the story.

Here's a Sample Task and Grade A* answer

Write, in any form, about three objects you would choose to put in a time capsule, to be recovered in 50 years time. Write about why you chose these objects.

Interesting opening, makes the piece feel more personal.

Alliteration and interesting vocab make the description very vivid.

Lovely metaphor.

It assumed a disproportionate importance, this task — three objects that would sum me up. Three objects that would symbolise the rich tapestry of my life, so that a stranger, fifty years hence, would feel as though he knew me.

First into the bundle went my named, wirebound 'School Organiser'. An obvious choice, perhaps, but after all, a record of the major events of my life. Classes, exams, merits and detentions, certainly; but more interesting are the page-margin doodles and scribbles: a pen-and-paper monument to every girl I've loved this year, notes from friends, a sketch of a soaring hawk, drawn during a deathless PSHE video session.

Next, and arguably as fundamental, was my mp3 player, the soundtrack to my life. Every lyric telling a new chapter, every melody etched into my soul, so that for years to come each time I hear an opening chord it will trigger a particular memory, as vivid as if it had only just happened. It seems almost unbelievable that when this music is next heard, I'll be in my late sixties, my life a series of paths already trodden and choices already made.

Using a variety of sentence structures shows that the writer is in control.

List of three adds rhythm.

Nice imagery.

Glossary

account	A written description of an <u>event</u>.
alliteration	Where the sounds in a phrase are repeated. It's often used to make a phrase stand out. E.g. "the <u>b</u>old, <u>b</u>rash <u>b</u>eat of the <u>b</u>and".
anecdote	A little real-life story which involves <u>you</u> or another person.
assertion	Presenting <u>opinions</u> as if they were <u>facts</u>.
audience	The people who will <u>read</u> a piece of writing.
bias	Giving <u>more support</u> to one point of view than to another, due to the writer's <u>own</u> <u>opinions</u> affecting the way they write.
colloquialism	An <u>informal</u> word or phrase that would normally be used in <u>conversation</u>. E.g. "Stop wittering on about it."
complex sentence	Two or more simple sentences joined to make one sentence using a <u>comma</u>. E.g. "When the cat came in, the dog left the room."
compound sentence	Two simple sentences joined to make one sentence using the word "<u>and</u>" or "<u>or</u>". E.g. "The cat came in and the dog left the room."
connectives	Words that help you <u>start sentences</u> in different ways, e.g. "however", "additionally".
contrast	When two things are described in a way which emphasises <u>how different</u> they are. E.g. a writer might contrast two different places, or two different attitudes.
counter-argument	The <u>opposite</u> point of view to the writer's own view. This is useful for arguing a point — first give the counter-argument, then <u>disagree</u> with it.
emotive	Language that has an <u>emotional</u> effect on the reader, e.g. the phrase "horrific scenes of carnage" will make the reader feel angry and disgusted.
empathy	When someone feels that they <u>understand</u> what someone else is experiencing and how they <u>feel</u>.
exaggeration	Describing something as <u>more</u> than it really is. E.g. "A million miles from home".
form	The <u>type</u> of text, e.g. a letter, a speech or a magazine article.
generalisation	A statement that gives an <u>overall impression</u>, sometimes a misleading one, without going into details. E.g. "Children today eat too much junk food."
homophones	Words that <u>sound</u> the same, e.g. "there" and "their".
imagery	Descriptive language that creates a <u>picture in your mind</u>, bringing the text to life.
irony	Saying one thing but <u>meaning the opposite</u>. E.g. "What a great idea of mine to go for a nice long walk on the rainiest day of the year."
language	The <u>choice of words</u> used. The language determines the effect the piece of writing will have on the reader, e.g. it can be emotive or persuasive.
metaphor	A way of describing something by saying that it <u>is something else</u>, to create a vivid image. E.g. "His eyes were deep, black, oily pools."
narrative	A part of a text that tells a <u>story</u> or describes an <u>experience</u>.
objective	A <u>neutral</u>, <u>unbiased</u> style of writing which contains <u>facts</u> rather than opinions.
onomatopoeia	A word that <u>imitates</u> the sound it represents when you say it, e.g. "<u>whisper</u>".

Glossary

P.E.E.D.	This stands for point, evidence, explanation, development. This means that for certain answers, you should make a <u>point</u>, give <u>evidence</u> to back it up, <u>explain</u> it properly and then <u>develop</u> your point.
personification	A special kind of description where you write about something as if it's a <u>person</u> or <u>animal</u>. E.g. "The sea growled hungrily."
pun	A "play on words" — a word or phrase that's deliberately used because it has <u>more than one meaning</u>. E.g. "She lies on the couch", where "lies" could mean "lies down" or "tells lies".
purpose	The <u>reason</u> someone writes a text. E.g. to persuade, to argue, to advise.
quotation	Exactly what someone said, which is added to a piece of writing using <u>speech marks</u>. E.g. The prime minister was heard to say "there's no problem", about the crisis.
repetition	Technique of <u>repeating</u> words (often three times) for effect.
rhetorical question	A question which <u>doesn't need an answer</u> and tries to persuade the reader to agree with the writer. E.g. "Are we really expected to put up with this government's lies?"
rule of three	Using <u>three</u> points or adjectives together to make an argument sound more effective. E.g. "It was a cold, dark and stormy night."
sarcasm	Saying something in a cutting, <u>nasty</u> way, often using <u>irony</u>. E.g. "Well done Kerry — another failed exam. You really are a bright spark."
satire	A text that makes fun out of someone or something in an attempt to <u>damage their reputation</u>. It's often done by imitating someone and exaggerating their flaws.
simile	A way of describing something by <u>comparing</u> it to something else, usually by using the word "like" or "as". E.g. "He was as pale as the moon."
slang	Words or phrases that sound <u>informal</u> or <u>conversational</u>, e.g. "bloke", "telly".
statistics	<u>Figures</u> from research, which are added to a piece of writing to <u>back up</u> points. E.g. "80% of parents agree that school uniform is too expensive."
structure	The <u>order</u> and <u>arrangement</u> of a piece of writing. E.g. how the text begins, develops and ends, whether it uses subheadings or not, etc.
style	The <u>way</u> a text is <u>written</u>, e.g. the type of language and techniques used.
subheading	A word or phrase that <u>stands out</u> from the text and <u>divides</u> the text into chunks. It gives an idea of what the <u>next section</u> of text is about.
subjective	A style of writing which has an <u>opinionated</u>, <u>personal</u> point of view.
superlatives	Phrases that use the word "<u>most</u>" or words that have "-<u>est</u>" at the end. E.g. "the most exciting holiday", "the hungriest crocodile".
tenses	Writing about the <u>past</u>, <u>present</u> or <u>future</u>. E.g. "I walked" is the past tense, "I walk" is the present tense and "I will walk" is the future tense.
theme	An <u>idea</u> or <u>topic</u> that's important in a piece of writing. E.g. a story could be based on the theme of forgiveness.
tone	The <u>mood</u> of a piece of writing, e.g. happy, sad, serious, lighthearted. It's an overall effect, created by things like choice of words, imagery and layout.
vocabulary	The range of <u>words</u> used.

Index